Graced 2 Grace

Graced
2
Grace

Why God Graces Us

Dr. H. Wallace Webster

RESOURCE *Publications* • Eugene, Oregon

GRACED 2 GRACE
Why God Graces Us

Copyright © 2015 H. Wallace Webster. All rights reserved. Except for brief quotations in critical publications or reviews, no part of this book may be reproduced in any manner without prior written permission from the publisher. Write: Permissions. Wipf and Stock Publishers, 199 W. 8th Ave., Suite 3, Eugene, OR 97401.

Resource Publications
An Imprint of Wipf and Stock Publishers
199 W. 8th Ave., Suite 3
Eugene, OR 97401

www.wipfandstock.com

ISBN 13: 978-1-4982-1866-5

Manufactured in the U.S.A.   04/29/2015

All scripture references, unless otherwise indicated, are from the King James version of the Bible.

Scripture references marked NKJV are from The Holy Bible: Containing the Old and New Testaments, New King James Version. Nashville: Nelson Bibles, 2006.

Contents

Acknowledgements and Dedication | vii

Introduction | ix

1 Getting Our Head Around Grace | 1
2 Understanding How We Have Been Graced Spiritually | 18
3 Understanding How We Have Been Graced Temporally | 38
4 We Have Been Graced to Grace Others | 56
5 Grace Must Be Applied | 72
6 Scriptural Reminders to Keep Grace on Track | 86
7 Barriers to Grace Living | 97
8 Benefits of Grace Living | 107
9 Be a Difference Maker | 117
10 Concluding Thoughts | 135

Appendix 1—Grace Throughout The New Testament | 137
Appendix 2—One-Another Ministry | 141

Bibliography | 143

Acknowledgements and Dedication

There are so many who deserve recognition for this work beyond me and I wanted to take a few moments to express my gratitude to them.

First and foremost, I want to thank my God and Savior. Without Him saving me, I would have no understanding at all as to what grace is all about.

Second, I want to thank my family. I was blessed to grow up in a home that frequently extended grace to me. Seeing grace in action inspired me to take up this search. Thank you David and Nora (parents), Neil, Chris, and Tim (siblings), Horace (whom I am proudly named after) and Irene (grandparents), and Stan and Gert (uncle and aunt). We all lived right next to each other growing up—what a blessing! My wife, Vicky, extends grace to me daily, otherwise I would not be here. My four daughters (Jessica, Jennifer, Kirsten, and Katelyn) have been great reminders to me of grace. The beauty and grace of these five women in my life cannot be measured.

Third, I want to thank my church family. I look out every Sunday and see a host of beautiful and grace like people that are certainly a joy to my heart.

Fourth, I cannot express in words the grace extended to me by my editor, Heather Bronner. Now there is a woman of grace who has to deal with my preachy style of writing!

Finally, I would like to dedicate this book to two men who will forever be a picture of grace to me. While they were both new believers and near the end of their lives here on earth, these two men impacted me greatly as beautiful examples of grace and blessing. They walked by my side, loved

Acknowledgements and Dedication

me, encouraged me, and blessed me. These two men both faced terminal cancer when I first met them, and I was able to walk their last hours with them on this earth.

First, I want to dedicate this book to Bob Stoesser. Cancer may have taken him, but his memory remains. He was there for me in many situations, and I still remember being in his house during his last hours. I also remember the night he prayed to receive Jesus. He went quietly into the presence of the Lord, and I can't wait to be with him again. I still miss him dearly. My second dedication is to Jim Claxton. I remember when he first came to our church, and his conversion to Jesus. These men, though new believers, taught me more than I taught them. Jim attended our three-year intensive discipleship program while taking chemo. He never missed a class, never missed a lesson, and never missed a memory verse (about 175 or so). Jim and Bob both had a way to light up a room. They knew no strangers. They were able to make everyone feel like they were their best friends. I often think of them and often wish they were still here. But they are truly in a far better place. So, when I think of grace, outside of my family and our Lord, these two men modeled it the best for me. I pray that my journey will grace others as these two have graced me. I love you men and miss you, and I look forward to worshipping by your side one day soon!

Dr. H. Wallace Webster

Introduction

Over the past several years, God has greatly convicted me concerning the subject of this book. As I have shared some of these thoughts with my congregation, I have noticed that others shared the same convictions. Many who have heard me share some of these truths have agreed with me that this is a journey worth examining further. Let me explain how I arrived at this particular location on my walk with the Savior.

It probably started in 1998 with a mission trip to Belarus. I certainly did not see myself as anyone who has much earthly treasure, but after seeing the lives of believers in this country, I began to examine my worldly kingdom a little differently. By American standards, I was probably considered lower middle class. We had four children, a reasonable house, and cars with a fair number of miles on them. Our children often got clothes from others who shared, and we lived modestly in suburban America. But as I examined these brothers in Belarus, it seemed like I was more like an upper-class person. These believers had *very* little. They had little refrigeration and went to the market daily. Few had a vehicle at all, and when I had the privilege to be in one of their homes, I saw it was very modest according to American standards. We went out to find a restaurant one night, and it was a task just to find a place that was open and fitting to go inside. I remember going that night into a warehouse-like area and wondering if it was a trap for unwary travelers. There were no signs and surely no restaurant to be found. After walking for moments (which seemed like hours), we

Introduction

entered a modest-looking restaurant and there enjoyed a respectable meal. Once again, by U.S. standards, this was sub-par.

Later, during this same trip, I was able to have dinner with a pastor who eagerly shared his home and food with us. We actually went to an abandoned army barrack that had been "renovated" for apartments. I remember passing statues and military equipment and wondering to myself if this was even a safe place! Eventually we arrived on the second floor of this barrack and were greeted by his wife and several children. There were a total of five people living there, and the complete size of the apartment could only have been about 400 square feet. The kitchen was barely able to fit one person, and the bathroom looked smaller! Two other rooms, hidden by curtains, were the bedrooms. Outside the kitchen was a small sitting room. I saw no table or dining room, yet we were invited to dinner. When dinner arrived, the host pulled a table from behind a sofa and set it up. We then sat on whatever we could around this small table and had a meal served to us. The meal was modest and we had wonderful fellowship. As we left, our translator explained that we had been treated as kings. That was probably the best meal the family had had for months, and the expense might have finished their budget that month. I quickly reached into my pocket and gave him some money to give to this family. Once again I saw how rich I was.

Travel in other countries has forced me to continue to redefine the words *rich* and *class*. I have seen the people in Chile who live in cardboard houses and makeshift homes that would cause many of us to shiver at their precarious construction. I have traveled the streets of Moscow, the Czech Republic, India, Indonesia, Brazil, Haiti, and Sri Lanka only to find the same story over and over. I was able to visit a ministry in India called the Matri Project. These kind and loving believers every day drive into a major city in India and pick up small children wandering the streets. The children are too poor to go to school, so they wander along the city begging for food. This ministry picks up the kids and takes them to a modest abode for ministry purposes. The children are bathed, clothed, fed, and taught about Jesus. What a trip that was for my wife and I! We drove up a "road" that was like a mountain climb. There were holes bigger than the vehicle, and cliffs that caused me to wonder where they were even taking us? Then our driver climaxed the whole experience by saying we must exit the car fast and get into the "building" before we were seen. It truly was an experience right out of a movie! And let me remind you the building was not as nice as some of our sheds.

Introduction

Once again we were welcomed and treated with dignity as if we were royalty. Trust me, my only royalty is the fact that I belong to the King of Kings, but they responded as if I was an earthly member of royalty. It was a deeply moving experience.

In another trip to India, I had the privilege of teaching several hundred Indian pastors who taught me far more than I taught them. I sat down with 30 pastors who had recently been the victims of violent attacks by Hindus in the Orissa area. I saw their scars and heard their stories. Some had lost family members and many had seen their churches burned to the ground. You should have heard these 30 men sing their praise to the Lord! They had even made up a song after that experience. At the end of the conference, the men began to pile out of the meeting room into vehicles waiting for them. I saw very few vehicles and wondered how they were going to travel. Twenty-five men piled into one pickup truck standing up! They would travel that way, some for nine or ten hours, back to their home. Once again I was reminded of how much we have and how much we are rich compared to much of the world.

This past summer, I was asked to preach a series of messages for a fall Bible conference. I was going to have plenty of time during the day for rest and preparation, so I decided to read a few books. I imagined that I was invited to this conference to be a blessing to the people, but when the conference was over, I think the people were not God's overall plan; I was. One of the books I read was David Platt's book, *Radical*. It is a book every Christian must read. It was the culmination of about a 15-year journey for me that was going to have life-long impact. Platt reminded me of just what I had been experiencing during the last few years of my life; now what was I to do with it?

In January of 2014, I began a series at our church on the widow's mites. It led me into a series called "Graced 2 Grace and Blessed 2 Bless." God had finally solidified some principles of His blessing to me that I could not deny. This book is my journey through what God has explained to me about why He has blessed us so richly. My prayer is that you would discover these truths as well as you journey with me to understanding the grace of God and our response to His grace. May we never be the same after this journey.

A few thoughts about the title: *Graced 2 Grace*. The reason I have the number 2 included in the title is that in order for grace to be effectual, it actually needs two parties. We already have the first and most important component to that equation: God. He is the "Gracer" and He has graced

INTRODUCTION

all in amazing ways, as we will see in our journey through these pages. But who will be the second party? All He is looking for is someone who would be willing to be a recipient and courier of His grace. I wonder, would I qualify? Would you? Would you be willing to walk these grace pages and allow God to stir you about being a grace agent for His glory? I believe it is a journey that will have eternal value.

Before I leave this introduction, I need to add one further truth. Remember the stories above about believers all over the world who have very little? They had one thing that very few American believers have—joy. It seems like there is a simple truth here for us to consider; the more we have of an earthly measure, the less the joy of the Lord. The more we posses of the treasures of this world, the more our hearts are grabbed for the non-eternal. Maybe America is not the place of the greatest blessing after all?

CHAPTER 1

Getting Our Head Around Grace

Understanding the Meaning of Grace

Grace. Such a misunderstood word. For many people, grace is something one says at holiday meal times, sort of an acknowledgment that some higher power had something to do with the food. Others feel it is something God gives us when we have been especially good or pleasing to him. There are also those who think that grace might just be something we get when our own efforts aren't enough.

Of all the people on the face of the earth who should understand grace, you would think it would be Christians. After all, grace is a "God-thing," so Christians should have a handle on it, right? Yet the more I journey through this life, the more I realize that most of us haven't fully grasped the concept of grace. Honestly, we can't understand how we have been graced until we know what *grace* really means. So let's start off with a definition of grace to help us lay some of those misconceptions to rest.

Looking at Grace Seriously

There are more descriptions of grace than are necessary for our study. I want to focus on just two which help define it so that we can see how we have been graced by God. The first is *common grace*. That is "a term theologians use to describe the goodness of God to all mankind universally."[1] Every human being who has lived or whoever will live, regardless of their plight on this earth, is to some level a recipient of this grace. In short, theologians agree that everyone in all of time has been graced by God. The important point isn't what the grace looks like, but the very fact that it exists universally.

The second part of our grace discussion is *saving grace*. That is the act of God whereby he saves those who, by believing, put their faith and trust in him and him alone. He is the Savior and it is by faith through grace that we are saved (Eph 2:8–9). All of mankind receives his universal common grace; only those who are believers receive the saving grace.

With these two thoughts in mind, we see that grace is "undeserved blessing freely bestowed on man by God—a concept which is at the heart not only of Christian theology but also of all genuinely Christian experience"[2] There are several key words in this definition that need further examination. One is undeserved; which means that there was no merit in mankind to prompt God to act graciously towards us. Man has done nothing to cause God to be gracious. His grace is that which is fully at his disposal and available only by his thought and plan. He chooses to be gracious. Let us permit God to speak on his own behalf as he communicated with Moses long ago: "And He said, I will make My goodness pass before thee, and I will proclaim the name of the Lord before thee, and *will be gracious to whom I will be gracious*, and will show mercy on whom I will show mercy" (Ex 33:19, italics mine). God does not change, so we can be sure that any truth about God's character is constant and steadfast. The same thought is repeated in the New Testament as Paul quotes from Ex 33:19 in Rom 9:15. Grace from God to mankind is an act that God alone determines, plans, and directs.

The second word in the definition for grace that should be explained is the word *freely*. This word emphasizes that God expects precisely nothing from man in order to for man to receive grace. Just as we must understand that grace is underserved, we need to comprehend that grace comes fully vested in God's goodness and desire to give. It comes freely. Let's look at a few verses that emphasize this further:

- Hosea 14:4—"I will love them freely"
- Romans 3:24—"being justified freely"

---

1. John MacArthur, *The Love of God* (Dallas: Word Publishing, 1996) 117.
2. Walter Elwell, *Evangelical Dictionary of Theology* (Grand Rapids: Baker Book House, 1984) 479.

- Romans 8:32— "how shall He not with him also freely give us all thing"
- 1 Corinthians 2:12—"that we might know the things that are freely given to us of God"
- Revelation 21:6—"I will give unto him that is athirst of the fountain of water of life freely"
- Revelation 22:17—"And whosoever will, let him take the water of life freely"

These are incredible descriptions of our God and his grace. No wonder it is called "amazing"! Just think of the depth of his riches that he has bestowed upon us, all because he determined to do so! It is just like he explained through Moses in Deut 7:7-8a "The Lord did not set His love upon you, nor choose you, because you were more in number than any people; for you were the fewest of all. But because the Lord loved you." God chose to display grace on Israel because of God and he did it freely as a demonstration of his love. It is freely given because it flows from the One who is the Gracious God. And every follower of Jesus is a rich recipient of his unfathomable grace, given to a people that do not deserve it and who are able to receive it freely. That is grace.

Some have also defined grace by using the actual word grace and putting it in an acrostic from: God's Riches At Christ's Expense (GRACE). In some ways that defines it well because it puts the entire burden of grace on the shoulders of Christ, who shouldered the cross for us. That, my friends, is grace.

Looking at Grace Statistically

I would imagine the majority of people who read this book will be among those most temporally graced by God. Before you begin looking at your position and your finances, remember to measure them accurately. Think about this: how many people in the world know Jesus in a personal saving way? Jesus reminds us that this won't be the majority of people:

- Matthew 7:13—"Enter in at the narrow gate; for wide is the gate, and broad is the way that leads to destruction, and many there be who go in that way;

- Matthew 7:14—"Because narrow is the gate, and hard is the way, which leads to life, and few there be that find it."

Now I realize Jesus gave no percentages here, but it would not be hard to determine that there are many more without Christ than with him. Many say that they know him, when in fact they do not (Matt 7:21–23). Therefore, I suggest that the percentage of believers is actually much smaller than the world likes to imagine. Let's offer an arbitrary 10 percent, which seems like a reasonable number and does justice to Jesus' words. Americans (who comprise the majority of the audience for this book), are only 300 million people in a world made up of 6 to 7 billion people. Therefore, I believe it is not stretching the picture to say if you live in America and are a believer, you may very well be part of a very small minority of the world's population. That, my friends, is a picture of a people who have greatly been blessed. Living in the most blessed country in the world with the greatest truth of all certainly makes us the most graced people on earth (or does it?).

Let's look at being blessed a little further with some statistics about things we often take for granted such as, water, food, shelter, etc. Look at these statistics from Richard Stearns' book, *The Hole in Our Gospel*:[3]

- Roughly 1 of 4 children in developing countries is underweight
- Some 350 to 400 million children are hungry
- About 1 in 7 worldwide – 854 million – do not have enough food to sustain them
- Approximately 25,000 people die each day of hunger or its related causes – about 9 million per year

How few of us ever worry about food or drinking water. Yet many of us, who represent the smallest fraction of the world, have these blessings and hoard them.

Looking at Grace Sensibly

Yes, I understand that some of this evaluation is relative. A man who is accustomed to driving a Mercedes may find it hard to see that driving a Dodge Neon is a blessing. A woman who is used to living in a 10-bedroom house may find living in a small efficiency apartment a far cry from

3. Richard Stearns, *The Hole in Our Gospel* (Nashville: Thomas Nelson, 2009) 135.

being blessed. Yet there are literally millions of people (maybe billions), who would see driving an old Dodge Neon with 200,000 miles and living in a one-bedroom efficiency as living a life of luxury. As a matter of fact, if they lived anywhere with a roof over their head and a vehicle to drive, they would think they were living the high life! As Americans, we tend to evaluate our status by our country alone; we see the Bill Gates and Donald Trumps as the measurement and then work our way down. But this type of man makes up such a minute percentage of the world's population. It would be wise for us as American followers of Jesus to see our position from more of a global view. I believe that is a more fair representation of our position on this planet. If you're not sure about how that could be, look a little bit deeper with me.

Graced to Be Alive

I am not sure we even understand just how gracious it was of God to give us a privilege to live on this earth. Yes, you may have had your share of pains and struggles, but to live on this earth and have that chance to be a part of his overall plan is a tremendous gift of grace. Every breath we breathe is an act of grace. We have all heard the adage, "Better to have loved and lost than never to have loved at all." I personally agree with that thought, and I would add that it's better to have lived and suffered, than never to have lived at all. And our amount of suffering living in America overall is insignificant compared to the world's suffering.

We get the privilege to live, have a chance to enjoy and experience what we can, and even if it comes with much pain, what is the other option—not to live at all? Some people, of course, have such great levels of pain that they do not even think living has been worth it. I am sorry for the real pain they carry. My prayer is that they would get to see life through the lenses of his eyes and understand that our God loves you and works all things out according to his will and our good. We must learn to trust him. For all of us, it would be wise to pause right now and just thank God for the grace that allowed us to live no matter how few and difficult the days may be. Better to have lived than not to live. Here is a sample prayer that you may consider:

> *God, thank you for allowing me the opportunity to live as a guest in your world. I don't even deserve the breath that I breathe daily and yet you permit that and so much more. I thank you for giving*

me eyes to see, ears to hear, and all the other manifold blessings that I take for granted. If I would just get my eyes off of what I think I should have and instead bless you for what You have given me, I would develop a spirit of praise that is worthy of you and I would be empowered to live out the true grace life. Father, I am frail. Please give me a grace view of you and a grace view of how I have been graced. I promise if you do, then I will be the grace vessel you have called me to be. Your servant.

Graced to Know God

Just imagine for a moment how unknowable God is with our limits. He is beyond human comprehension with transcendent beauty, glory, and majesty. Yet he allows puny and insignificant mankind to know him. So the psalmist cries out, "What is man that you are mindful of him, and the son of man, that you visit him?" (Ps 8:4). His point: what are we to God? Yet he allows us the privilege of knowing him, even to the point that Paul modeled a prayer for us in Phil 3:10 "that I may know him." God is only knowable because he allows us to know him. He has revealed himself in the world around us and in his Word. He permits us to come and know him and taste and see that he is amazing. This truth is available to all, and those who know him in this way are so graced! Have you thanked him lately for this grace to you? Take the time to do so once again!

Graced in Ways We Often Take for Granted

By now, I trust you realize that all we have and all we are is provided through his grace. Take a moment now and write on the page provided here just how you see you have been graced. Some suggestions might be: family, friends, job, eyes, education, things you have experienced so far in life, places you have traveled, different foods, or even good drinking water.

Getting Our Head Around Grace

Put your list here:

Another thing you can do is look back and see how many times God has spared you from problems, pain, and difficult situations. There are probably many you may not even see, but there are likely some you remember or have locked in your mind. Think about babies born to moms who couldn't have children, jobs that came out of nowhere, illnesses that the doctors said would last and yet disappeared, and car accidents that nearly happened. Please use the accompanying space below to list his many graces to you. Read this old hymn as you prepare:

Count Your Many Blessings[4]

When upon life's billows you are tempest tossed,
When you are discouraged, thinking all is lost,
Count your many blessings name them one by one,
And it will surprise you what the Lord hath done.

Count your blessings, name them one by one;
Count your blessings, see what God hath done;
Count your blessings, name them one by one,
And it will surprise you what the Lord hath done.

Are you ever burdened with a load of care?
Does the cross seem heavy you are called to bear?
Count your many blessings, every doubt will fly,
And you will be singing as the days go by.

When you look at others with their lands and gold,
Think that Christ has promised you His wealth untold.
Count your many blessings, money cannot buy
Your reward in heaven, nor your Lord on high.

4. Hymn: "When upon Life's Billows You Are Tempest Tossed." Hymnalnet RSS. Accessed May 8, 2014.

> So amid the conflict, whether great or small,
> Do not be discouraged, God is over all;
> Count your many blessings, angels will attend,
> Help and comfort give you to your journey's end.

Put your list here.

Looking at Grace Specifically

Maybe it would be to our advantage to add some more specifics to our definition of grace. Often we discuss things adamantly with others without realizing we are using different definitions of the same word. I suspect that may be the case with grace. It reminds me of the story of the man who had his sofa stuck in his exterior door of his house. His neighbor saw his look of despair and ran over to assist. The neighbor was a rather muscular man and so the man welcomed his assistance. After about 15 minutes with no progress, the neighbor scratching his head told the man that he was not sure the sofa would get through the door into his house. The man replied, "Into the house? I am trying to get it out of the house!" The neighbor was well-intentioned, but the two men were not on the same page. Let me take a few moments to put us all on the same page with all the terms we will use in this book

Defining Mercy

The word "mercy" expresses a concept similar to grace. Very simply, grace is giving us what we don't deserve, and mercy is not giving us what we do deserve. You can see readily that these two are basically inseparable. Paul understood the importance of these two truths as he included them in all three introductions to his pastoral epistles:

- 1 Timothy 1:2—"grace, mercy, and peace, from God our Father"
- 2 Timothy 1:2—"grace, mercy, and peace from God, the Father"
- Titus 1:4—"grace, mercy, and peace from God, the Father"

Ryrie explains mercy this way: "Mercy is that aspect of His goodness that causes God to show pity and compassion."[5] Goodness is just another way to say "grace." Mercy is that aspect of his grace that causes God to show pity and compassion. Maybe we could summarize it this way: God, in his amazing grace, looked down upon mankind, and out of this grace, determined to apply mercy to a people that were deserving of his full wrath and judgment. Grace is the cause and mercy is the application.

Defining Justice

In order to see grace and mercy in their proper dimension, it is worthwhile to take a brief look at his justice. God is a holy God. Scripture demonstrates that for us in both the Old and New Testaments (Isa 6:3, Rev 4:8). Because he is holy, he has no tolerance for sin. Sin cannot stand in his presence. We will look later at the extremity of our sin, but for now just accept that mankind stands before God as totally depraved and absolutely unworthy of any grace or mercy. The man who sins will die (Rom 6:23), and this death is two-fold: physical death which happens to all people; and spiritual death, separation from God forever. This is the fate of all mankind from the sin of Adam (Rom 5:12). God's holiness and man's sinfulness bring God's justice into action. Sin must be accounted for to a holy God who is righteous and just to bring about full wrath on mankind for this sinful condition. We deserve this wrath and justice. Instead, God sends his Son through his grace and extends to us forgiveness as demonstrated by his mercy. While we will cover this in greater depth later on, if you are a believer in Jesus, I suggest you put this book down and fall on your face to this holy God and praise him for the fact that justice was served on his Son so you could enjoy his grace and mercy. Tears are flowing down my face even as I write this. We deserved wrath and justice, but Jesus stepped in and took it all for us. Paul says it so well in 2 Cor 5:21: "For He has made him who knew no sin, to be sin for us, that we might be made the righteousness of God in him."

5. Charles Ryrie, *Basic Theology* (Wheaton: Victor Books, 1986) 44.

Defining Forgiveness

One component of his grace and mercy is the enjoyment we have in forgiveness. As sinners, we deserved his justice and wrath. But instead we are forgiven. If grace is giving us what we don't deserve, and mercy is not giving us what we do deserve, then forgiveness is giving us a standing in full pardon.

Forgiveness might be looked at as the receipt after grace and mercy have been applied. Forgiveness has three dimensions. There is *positional forgiveness* that gives us the right to be a part of his family. He has to see us as holy as he is to be accepted, and when Jesus took our place, we became partakers of that which gives us the right standing before God. First Corinthians 1:30 explains, "But of Him are you in Christ Jesus, who of God is made unto us wisdom, and righteousness, and sanctification (holy), and redemption." Once pardoned, we are declared positionally forgiven; we can never lose this forgiveness.

But as we all know, we mess up. Therefore we need *practical forgiveness*. That is why John reminds us in 1 John 1:9 to confess our sins for this daily forgiveness. Finally, one day we will be *permanently forgiven*. We receive all of this because grace flowed from the heart of our Gracious God and Savior to us, his creation.

Hopefully you can see that the grace God shows us is so vast that there is no way to measure its greatness. Therefore it is best to simply understand that you are what you are by the grace of God, and for that you have much reason to boast in your God. The question remains—what have you done with his grace?

Defining Redemption

There is one more term that I believe needs definition at this time: *redemption*. Redemption basically means that we have been purchased. What a thought! I remember watching a movie about Hosea, the Old Testament prophet, and seeing him buy a woman who was basically a harlot, redeeming her for himself. It was moving. The picture is reminiscent of what our Savior has done for us. There we were, being auctioned off on the slavery shopping block, and he came along and redeemed us for no reason whatsoever other than to pour grace on us. He took us to himself, washed us, cleansed us, dressed us, and treated us as sons. How can we miss the depth of his grace to us?

Understanding the God of Grace

Grace in the Old Testament

Many people believe that grace is a New Testament concept. I have frequently heard assertions that the Old Testament if full of hate and wrath and the New Testament is love and grace. Yet these are just not factually accurate. First, grace is an attribute of God, and since God cannot change, there must be grace from the beginning. And yes there is. The word *grace* occurs 38 times, *gracious* 28 times, and *graciously* four times. That is a total of 70 times in the English text of the Old Testament that the word grace appears. Clearly, grace is an Old Testament concept. The Lord graced mankind to even allow the world to exist. Then he graced man to be the chief of the created order. And this was just the beginning of how it was poured out all through the Old Testament.

- Genesis 1:1—"In the beginning, God created . . . " He is grace in the very beginning.
- Genesis 6:8—"Noah found grace in the eyes of the Lord" (which is also the first time it appears in the Old Testament).
- Psalm 84:11—"the Lord will give grace and glory"
- Proverbs 3:34—"but He gives grace to the lowly"
- Exodus 34:6—"And the Lord passed before him and proclaimed, The Lord, Lord God, merciful and gracious, long-suffering, and abundant in goodness and truth." Here in the second book of the Old Testament God reveals himself as "gracious." It is one of his early titles for who he wants his people to know him by.

Of course many of the occurrences of grace in the Old Testament are not directly connected to God, yet the principles of grace that are included in the other passages emanate from the God of all grace. But when it comes to gracious, most of the occurrences are directly related to him:

- Exodus 22:27—"for I am gracious"–God describes himself
- Psalm 86:15— "a God full of compassion, and gracious"

- Psalm 111:4—"Lord is gracious and full of compassion"

It does not require an in-depth study of the Old Testament to see that God is full of grace and has been gracious since the very beginning of time. God cannot become more gracious. Grace is his character, and that is not something that can be increased or depleted. He was gracious to create. He was gracious to allow man to exist. He was gracious to allow Noah to experience grace and save mankind. He was gracious to call out Abram out of the land of idolatry. He was gracious to meet with his people, put his name on them, and give them the Law to guide them in their daily lives. He was gracious to protect his people as many nations tried to attack and destroy. Even when his people rebelled, he was gracious to respond when they called out to him. Notice in Judges and Kings how often God intervened when his people, although bringing evil upon themselves by sinful behavior, still acted in grace when they cried out. This God is our God of grace.

I would suggest his greatest display of grace in the Old Testament comes very early in Gen 3:15, when he promises Someone is coming to remedy man's mess. That promise continually appears throughout the Old Testament. Josh McDowell, in his book *The New Evidence that Demands a Verdict*,[6] suggests that the Old Testament offers 61 different prophecies about the coming of Jesus. Here are just a very few—think how hard these would be for anyone to fulfill!

- Born of a virgin
- House of David
- Bones not broken
- Heartbroken
- His side pierced
- Darkness over the Land
- Buried in rich man's tomb

In addition, many scholars suggest he is pictured in every book and hinted at all throughout the Old Testament. Jesus' appearance and life on this earth were our God's greatest display of grace, especially for a people who couldn't care less! To examine the Old Testament and not see grace that permeates it from cover to cover is a great disservice to the character of God.

6. Josh McDowell, *New Evidence that Demands a Verdict* (Nashville: Thomas Nelson, 1999).

Grace in the New Testament

Most people have no trouble seeing grace in the New Testament. It occurs some 156 times and the word for gifts (grace gifts) occurs an extra 17 times. That is not an insignificant number! As far as the books are concerned, 23 of the 27 New Testament books include the word *grace*. Matthew and Mark are the only writers who do not use the word *grace* in any of their writings; the other two books without the word are 1 and 3 John. Grace can be found very early in the New Testament when the angel tells Mary she has been found with favor (grace) from God in Luke 1:30, and John uses it in John 1:14, explaining that "he is full of grace and truth." Interestingly, the New Testament also closes with a statement of grace. As a matter of fact, it is the last verse of the Bible and the last verse penned by John under the inspiration of the Holy Spirit: "The grace of the Lord Jesus Christ be with you all. Amen." Preachers often close with a sentence like, "Now if you forget all that I have said up to this point, please remember this . . . ." The last statement is often the one we remember. That is why a great message always brings the main point home in the last few words. While we do not want to relegate Scripture to its last few words, I suspect that Rev 22:21 might just sum up the whole Bible. Jesus and grace are certainly the central theme of the Book. If someone sincerely wanted to know God and found Jesus and grace and understood these truths, would they not be on the right path?

The New Testament says many other things about grace:

- Romans 3:24—"justified freely by grace"
- Romans 5:2—"we have access by faith into this grace"
- Romans 5:15—"much more the grace of God and the gift by grace, which is by one man, Jesus Christ, has abounded unto many"
- Romans 5:20—"where sin abounded, grace did much more abound"
- Romans 6:14—"for you are not under the law, but under grace"
- 2 Corinthians 9:8—"God is able to make all grace abound toward you"
- Galatians 1:6—"that called you into the grace of Christ"
- Ephesians 2:5—"for by grace you are saved"

This is just a small sampling of the many great statements in the New Testament that pertain to a believer in Jesus. We, of all people, are the most blessed (graced) people on the face of the earth. Regardless of what comes our way, we have been graced.

The Apostle Paul might accurately be called the Apostle of Grace. Let me explain why I say this. Paul declares that he was the chief of sinners In his first epistle to Timothy, his son in the faith, Paul says, "This is a faithful saying, and worthy of all acceptance, that Christ Jesus came into the world to save sinners, of whom I am chief" (1 Tim 1:15). I like how MacArthur puts it: "Few could be considered a worse sinner than someone who blasphemed God and persecuted His church."[7] Jesus reminds us that the person who has been forgiven most, loves the most (Luke 7:47). By human measurements, Paul had been one of the greatest sinners; he had been forgiven much. No wonder he is the Apostle of Grace. In fact, I find it fascinating that in every book he wrote, Paul began and ended with an exhortation about grace. Notice these examples:

- Philippians 1:2—"Grace be unto you."
  Philippians 4:23—"The grace of the Lord Jesus Christ be with you all."

- Colossians 1:2—"Grace be unto you."
  Colossians 4:18—"Grace be with you. Amen"

Paul had a keen sense of the extent of grace necessary to save a sinner such as he was. Yet when we look closer as we will in a later section, we will see that we, too, have been greatly graced with the privilege of being called children of God. Maybe the reason many believers do not grace others is because they have not discovered just how much they have been graced. Do you understand the magnitude of grace to save a sinner such as yourself? Do you think it took amazing grace to save you?

The Names of God Display Grace

Dr. F.E. Marsh says that if you take the "El" names for God in the Bible and categorize them, you will see several qualities of God surface. One that he mentions is found in Jonah 4:2: "as to his compassion, he is the Gracious God."[8] In fact, Scripture uses this so frequently that it becomes one of God's titles or names. While some may argue that Grace is not an "official" name

---

7. John MacArthur, *MacArthur Study Bible* (Nashville: Thomas Nelson, 1997) 1861.

8. F.E. Marsh, *The Structural Principles of the Bible* (Grand Rapids: Pikering and Ingles, 1969).

of God, they must nevertheless acknowledge that his name is always a reflection of his character. Names given to God in the Bible include Provider, Savior, Wonderful, Counselor, etc. Thus, using "Gracious" as his name is perfectly consistent with his character and with Biblical tradition. I believe saying his name is Grace is a fair and accurate interpretation of Scripture.

- Exodus 22:27—"... I am gracious"
- Exodus 34:6—"And the Lord passed by before him, proclaimed, The Lord, Lord God, merciful and gracious..."
- Nehemiah 9:31—"... for you are a gracious and merciful God."
- Psalm 116:5—"Gracious is the Lord..."

When you think of God, especially if you think in terms of what he has done for you, it should be easy to call him gracious. Have you come to a place where his grace is what you see when you see him?

Understanding the Cost of Grace

Jesus Equals Grace

Jesus came to this earth as an extension of the grace of God. In his letter, Paul reminds Titus that the grace of God brings salvation (Tit 2:11). If you follow Jesus' life on the earth and evaluate his actions, you see this grace offered daily to others, and particularly in the physical and spiritual realms.

He Graced Others Physically

How often do you hear someone say that they are blessed (or graced)? It usually means that they have food, health, water, etc. Jesus supplied these to many while here on the earth. He graced people. He blessed people. For example, before we eat, we say grace; we thank him for providing the food for us. We see that as a blessing. Or if you get an answer to prayer, you may respond and say that God blessed you. Jesus did that and should receive the glory. "Every good and perfect gift comes from above" (Jas 1:17).

There is a long list of the blessed folks who lived during Jesus' time. There were times he fed multitudes and times when he just had food ready for a few (John 21:9-12). There were times they came to him all day and he healed them all: the lame, the blind, the deaf, the infirm, the hurting.

To claim Christianity is to see the importance of helping the less fortunate. Jesus modeled that for us. The New Testament is full of examples of Jesus gracing people physically. You cannot miss that if you read Matthew through John.

He Graced Others Spiritually

However, Jesus just did not grace others physically, and that is one of the many reasons that humanitarian relief alone is not an accurate representation of Christianity. We may need to feed the hungry on the front end, or dig wells in a village before presenting the Gospel, but to simply feed the hungry or give water to the thirsty alone is a poor substitute for Christ. All we have done is alleviated some earthly suffering, which is temporary, and allowed them to perish and suffer eternally. Salvation must accompany humanitarian relief. Jesus was salvation and he came to seek and save the lost (Luke 19:10). People who encountered Jesus were never the same.

Just think of how he graced others spiritually while here on the earth. First and foremost he changed lives. But he also chose the 12 and graced them with grace to grace others, and they did. They were called, discipled (graced by his teaching), and told to go out and live out that grace. Of course he graced more than just those men as he sent out the 70 and often taught the multitudes. Have we forgotten we are called to be like Jesus? Why would that not include gracing others?

Two words that are sometimes found with the word grace are the words *freely* (Rom 3:24, 5:15,16,18), and *given* (Rom 12:3,6; 13:15; 1 Cor 1:4). Grace is freely given to us by a Grace God, who is Gracious. This culminated when he hung on the cross for our sins. We will explain the depth of this grace in a later section, but let's make something clear. There is no way eternity is long enough for us to repay his grace to us. It is free, but it is not cheap, nor did it come cheaply. God required the death of his Son to make grace an active offer to mankind. Can you see the enormous debt of grace?

Hebrews 2:9 says "that He by the grace of God should taste death for every man." His death was a grace death. God sent him by grace and he came by grace. He offered his life as an extension of that grace so we all could partake of that which can only be acquired by the entrance of grace. His grace made the way, and it is offered freely for all to receive. Every time you hold the bread and wine in your hand, remember the cost, and

Getting Our Head Around Grace

remember that Jesus equals grace. In fact, let's just pause a moment and review his last few hours on this earth. Note the things that he suffered.

1. He was betrayed for the cost of a common criminal by a co-laborer.
2. He was denied by one of his closest followers.
3. All of his followers forsook and left him.
4. His own siblings had disowned him and Scripture tells of no family other than his mother during his last hours.
5. Beaten with rods, fists, and a whip that left him mutilated beyond description. Isaiah 52:14 says you could not even recognize him as a man when they were finished with him.
6. He was lied about.
7. He was spat upon.
8. He was humiliated.
9. He was forced to carry his cross. The word "excruciating" comes from the Latin, *excruciatus*, or "out of the cross." Jesus' death was that and much more.
10. He was crucified on a cross, something we cannot even comprehend.

There is no doubt that Jesus suffered greatly on that cross. There was the full impact of the pain of crucifixion, which is documented both by historians and present-day doctors. Then there was the thirst. The inability to breathe. The pain of nails, his back, the crown of thorns. Even worse, there was the spiritual battle where the Father placed all our sin on his Son. It is at that time he cried out "My God, My God, why have you forsaken me?" (Matt 27:46). He gave us his full measure of grace. What a cost. What a Savior.

So, do you have your head around grace now? Okay, maybe that's not a fair question, since I'm not sure any of us fully have our heads wrapped around the concept. But my prayer is twofold: first, that you have a better grasp of grace, and second, that you'll make it a lifelong journey. Grace is truly amazing.

CHAPTER 2

Understanding How We Have Been Graced Spiritually

IT IS IMPERATIVE FOR a child of God to see grace for what it is—unmerited favor. There is simply nothing we did to earn it, merit it, deserve it, or warrant it. Grace comes to us totally because of the one doing the gracing.

Grace answers all the important questions of life. Why am I here on this earth? I am here as an extension of his grace. What am I to do with my life? I live out his grace to others. Why do things happen to me the way that they do? They happen so that his grace will be mirrored in my life. Grace begins us and grace completes us. We will only begin to live out our life to the fullest when we understand grace.

- It is because of grace that I exist.
- It is because of grace that I live.
- It is because of grace that I have anything.
- It is because of grace that I am not heading to Hell.

It is grace from the beginning to the end, and it will be grace that leads us home. Just try to imagine the amount of grace necessary to cover our sin? Have you ever really considered just how much sin each person is accountable for?

Understanding How We Have Been Graced Spiritually

I remember a song we used to sing in our little country church, "Grace Greater Than All My Sin."[1] Here are the lyrics of this old hymn. Notice especially the chorus's last line, which mirrors the title. What a great truth! But do we really understand what that means?

> Marvelous grace of our loving Lord,
> Grace that exceeds our sin and our guilt!
> Yonder on Calvary's mount outpoured,
> There where the blood of the Lamb was spilled.
>
> Refrain:
>
> Grace, grace, God's grace,
> Grace that will pardon and cleanse within;
> Grace, grace, God's grace,
> Grace that is greater than all our sin!
>
> Sin and despair, like the sea waves cold,
> Threaten the soul with infinite loss;
> Grace that is greater, yes, grace untold,
> Points to the refuge, the mighty cross.
>
> Dark is the stain that we cannot hide;
> What can we do to wash it away?
> Look! There is flowing a crimson tide,
> Brighter than snow you may be today.
>
> Marvelous, infinite, matchless grace,
> Freely bestowed on all who believe!
> You that are longing to see His face,
> Will you this moment His grace receive?

Let's examine the specifics of what this means to each of us personally.

Grace Covers the Penalty of Sin

"For if we say we have no sin, we deceive ourselves, and the truth is not in us" (1 John 1:8). We all are sinners as the Bible clearly states, but that does not mean that we fully understand the depth of that sin. As a matter of fact, one of the reasons that many do not come to Christ for repentance is

---

1. "Grace Greater than Our Sin." HymnSite.com. January 1, 1911. Accessed September 2, 2014.

that they do not believe that they are "that bad" and in need of that much grace. They point to the rapist, the murderer, the jihadist, the terrorist, and conclude, "I am not that much of a sinner. Therefore why do I need a Savior?" We have been lulled to sleep—into a spiritual mindset that has lost the seriousness of total depravity. Just how bad off is mankind before a Holy God? Even if we have not sinned to the full extent that we could, there is no more sin that we could do that would separate us from God any more than we already are. We are in trouble. Let me explain.

First, we are sinners because of our birth. Now those of us who have had the privilege of holding a beautiful newborn in our arms, especially one that belongs to us, know that it is a joy that cannot be compared to any other early joy. I remember holding my firstborn. She was so beautiful to look at. Everything was perfect. She even scored a 10 on her APGAR test, so the doctors and nurses also thought she was perfect. Then we came home, and somehow she learned how to do wrong. I just didn't get it. She had such good role models. How could she do anything wrong? That is just it. Even if we were perfect parents and put her in a perfect home (which did not happen), she had something else working against her. She had a sin nature given to her by birth from Adam and from me, her dad.

One of the great doctrinal truths about Jesus is that he was born without this sin nature. How was that possible? He was virgin born. Sin is passed down by the man. Now ladies, enjoy this for all it's worth. Remember all the times he wanted to blame one of your children's behavior on you? Set the record straight. If you could have brought children into the world without him, your children would have been perfect. Well, maybe that's not fair, and it's certainly not possible—but with Jesus it was. That which was conceived in Mary was of the Holy Spirit (Luke 1:34–35). There are no more of those kinds of births available. It was a one and done deal. Therefore all children born before Jesus and after Jesus have to contend with what Paul explains in Rom 5:12 "Wherefore, as by one man (Adam – Gen 3), sin entered the world, and death by sin, and so death passed upon all men, for all have sinned." His point is that as Adam sinned in the Garden of Eden, so did I. When he sinned, he sinned on my behalf and the judgment that came upon him came upon all of mankind after that sin. Therefore, everyone born into this world is born into sin and born under the condemnation of death. And that death has both a spiritual and a physical dimension. Spiritual in that we are born separated from God, and physical in that we all are going to face the penalty of physical death. Because Adam sinned and I am born a son of Adam, I stand as a guilty sinner, separated from God, and worthy of eternal and physical separation from God.

- Romans 5:17—by one man (Adam), death reigned.
- Romans 5:18—by the one offense (Adam) judgment came upon all mankind [including you and me] to condemnation.

As I said earlier, this sin alone was enough to judge us eternally. Even if you lived this life without sin, or sinning "just a little," you are positionally declared an enemy of God (Rom 5:8–10), and deserving of a Christ-less eternity. We stand under the penalty of sin.

What does all this mean? Well, we were guilty enough by just being born into this world for God to declare us under judgment and condemnation, which condemned us to an eternity in Hell. Now do you think for one moment that God would declare that kind of punishment for someone who had not done a whole lot wrong? Can you imagine God opening up Hell's gates for people who have just messed up a little, sinned a little, done a few bad things, or just basically missed the mark? Not at all! Hell was actually prepared for the devil and his angels (Matt 25:41). For God to condemn mankind for simply being born and not doing anything wrong to have this positional judgment certainly clarifies that our depravity at birth was godless and full of the wrath of God. Those beautiful little cherubs that we bring home are simply condemned sinners waiting to act out that sin. And it doesn't take long for them to demonstrate. Unfortunately, we act out our sinful condition.

I want to digress for just a moment here to discuss the death of a child before the age of accountability. One of the great dilemmas we have concerns this positional condition that every child inherits. What about all the miscarriages, aborted babies, still born babies, and babies/small children who die before they can even articulate their faith? Does their condition demand that they be sent to Hell? This is not an easy question, and the Scriptures really do not develop this thought with enough detail to be adamant. But I have concluded that babies of this kind go on to Heaven. Without trying to explain, I would suggest you read John MacArthur's excellent treatment of this theme in his book *Safe in the Arms of God*. There are reasonable arguments to defend that we can expect to see our children again one day, safe in his arms. I trust this would encourage you that have had such a loss.

Second, not only are we sinners by birth, but we are sinners by choice. Please understand that committing a sin doesn't *make* us sinners, it *proves* we are sinners. "Man looks on the outward, but God looks on the heart" (1 Sam 16:7). And man's heart is "desperately wicked," according to Jer 17:9. So it doesn't matter whether we tell a lie or murder a person—it's only proving what is already true about us.

The most obvious example of this again is Adam. Adam's one sin was enough for God to judge him and punish him. What makes us think that our sin would be treated any less? He only ate an "apple." Is our sin less than that?

Romans 3:10 makes it clear that "there is none righteous, no not one." Notice it does not say that there are some mostly righteous, partially righteous, or close to righteous. Our activity as a sinner has put us in a condition of sinful behavior, and it only takes one sin to declare us a sinner. Romans 3:23 concludes that our sinful behavior makes us worthy of death. Romans 6:23 adds that this sin has offered us the wages of death.

Each of us stands before God positionally as a declared sinner and practically we enforce that concept by sinning in our daily lives. And all it took was one "little" sin to confirm that we are a sinner. For example, how many lies does a person have to tell to be called a liar? How many murders does a man need to commit to be a murderer? How many affairs does a man have to have to be called an adulterer? How many sins does a man have to commit to be declared by a Holy God that he is a sinner? The answer is *one*. If you have committed one sin, regardless of being born a sinner, you are a sinner. And that one sin is enough for our God to consign you to Hell for eternity. He cannot stand for sin to even be in his presence, regardless of how small.

It was sin that killed his Son. Our sin was on the Savior, and God had to turn his back on his only Begotten Son. Now you think that your one sin is insignificant? Ask God to help you see your sin as he does.

Third, not only are we sinners by birth and by choice, but we are also declared sinners by the standard of the Law. James 2:10 says, "For whosoever shall keep the whole law, and yet offend in one point, he is guilty of all." Let that soak in. We may decide we are not as wicked as a murderer, rapist, or other evil person. But that's irrelevant according to God's standards.

Matthew 5:27–28 talks about discerning sin even in our thoughts: "You have heard that it was said by them of old, you shall not commit adultery. But I say unto you have whosoever looks on a woman to lust after her has committed adultery with her already in his heart" (NKJV). The point is that many men will say, "I have not committed adultery," and yet this verse challenges not just the *act*, but the *thought*. Once again we are reminded that God knows what is in our hearts. We can deceive people, but we cannot deceive God.

If that example seems a little extreme to you, look at Matt 5:21–22: "You have heard that it was said by them of old, 'You shall not kill and whosoever shall kill shall be in danger of judgment.' But I say unto you that whoever is angry with his brother without a cause shall be in danger of judgment." You might confidently assert that you're not a murderer, but are you holding anger in your heart against someone?

But wait, it gets worse. According to Jas 2:10 (see above), this one thing now makes us guilty of breaking every law in the books. And, according to some who have actually counted the laws, this means 613 infractions. Now, can you imagine going to traffic court and trying to defend your case before the judge? Would you really want to try to argue that you have broken every traffic law (driving under the influence, vehicular manslaughter, leaving the scene of an accident), but he should let you off anyway? No judge is going to let you off the hook, for something that "small"! And the laws we are discussing are the moral laws of God, not something as simple as man's laws!

The combination of these three makes the penalty of sin enormous. We are sinners by birth, sinners by choice, and sinners for violating his Law. Any one of the above would declare us worthy of condemnation. Yet Jesus comes along and pays the entire debt in full. The book of Romans adds more to this discussion (italics mine):

- Romans 5:15—"But not as the offense, so also is the free gift. For if through the offense of one (Adam) many (all) are dead, *much more the grace* of God, and the gift by grace, which is by one man, Jesus Christ, has abounded unto many (some)." [We can conclude these interpretive additions by the whole of Scripture.]

- Romans 5:17—"For if by one man's offense (Adam) death reigned by one, much more they who receive *abundance of grace*, and of the gift of righteousness shall reign in life by one, Jesus Christ."

- Romans 5:20—"Moreover the law entered that the offense might abound, but where sin abounded, *grace did much more abound.*"

Criminals in Jesus' day would often have a written document, declaring why they were serving time, posted on their jail cell. When they completed their term, they would be able to take that document with them and show it to anyone who would question their release from debt. It would be like writing today across a bill of sale with these words: "paid in full." That is exactly what Jesus meant on the cross when he said, "It is finished." Paid in full. So every one of us who have declared Jesus as our Lord and Savior can show them our handwriting of ordinances what was against us and show the red blood letters that he paid for us (Col 2:14). You and I are sinners of the worst sort. Stop comparing yourself to those you consider "better" or "worse," and see yourself as God sees you. If you have never accepted Christ as your Savior, do it now. All it requires for you to do is bow your head and repent of the fact that you are a sinner worthy of Hell and ask him to save you for his glory. He will take you at your prayer.

Jesus truly paid it all, and all to him we owe. That is a picture of his grace that covers the penalty of all our sin. And he does not stop there.

Grace Covers the Power of Sin

Not only has he provided the grace to cover our sin in its entirety, he also has provided the grace necessary to deliver us from the power of sin. Sin is powerful. When we were in the condition of "B.C." (Before Christ—that is, prior to salvation), we had absolutely no power to resist sin. As the "great theologian" Oscar Wilde said, "I can resist anything but temptation." Honestly, that is the picture of you and me before Christ. We may not have sinned all that we could have sinned, but we have no power to stop sinning altogether. We are sinners and we demonstrate it regularly.

Keep in mind that there are two types of sin: sins of commission and sins of omission. We seem to focus mostly on the sins of commission, such as lying, stealing, murdering, etc. These are sins of commission; sins we commit. But the Bible addresses the forgotten area of sins of omission. Listen to what Jas 4:17 says: "Therefore to him that knows to do good, and does it not, to him it is sin." So even if we can boast of avoiding the sinful acts, can we truly boast that we always do what is good? Do you read your Bible daily, pray regularly, share the Gospel to the lost we come in contact with, and praise God for all things? What other things are we omitting that we know are right?

But there is good news. We don't have to give in to sin and the dominion of sin. He has conquered sin and given us the ability to have victory. Sin has been defeated and has no power to keep us in bondage. Now this does not mean we are sinless, but there is power available for us to sin less every day.

- Romans 6:6—"Knowing this, that our old man is crucified with him, that the body of sin might be destroyed, that henceforth we should not serve sin."
- Romans 6:11—"Likewise reckon you also yourselves to be dead indeed unto sin."
- Romans 6:12—"Let not sin therefore reign in your mortal body that you should obey it in its lusts."
- Romans 6:14—"For sin shall not have dominion over you; for you are not under the law, but under grace."

There it is. Grace comes in where sin abounded, and grace wipes the slate clear at the source so that resisting sin is not only possible, it is expected. There is no sin out there that can have dominion over us. Grace is greater than our sinful condition and our sinful practice. Marvelous grace of our loving Lord. And still there is more!

Grace Covers the Presence of Sin

Every believer out there who has battled with sin knows how draining and often discouraging that fighting sin can be. Unfortunately for many of us, sin wins more than it should. We long for the day when sin will be forever over. Great news—that day is coming! Scripture is clear that this is not all there is. There is a day coming that is not just some fairy tale of happily ever after, but a true eternal existence with God with no more sin.

Revelation 21:4 says, "And God shall wipe away all tears from their eyes; and there shall be no more death, neither sorrow, nor crying, neither shall there be any more pain; for the former things are passed away." Now although sin is not specifically stated in this verse, we know that if death has been done away with, so has sin, death's counterpart.

Revelation 21:27 adds, "But there shall by no means enter it anything that defiles, or cause an abomination or a lie." There is no room in Heaven for sin. The grace that covered our positional sinful condition from birth and practical sinful condition by actions will also one day cover the very presence of sin. What a day that will be, all because of Grace.

Scripture makes it clear that "Eye has not seen nor ear heard all that God has in store for us that are His followers" (1 Cor 2:9). He has so much more for us that we cannot even imagine.

Ephesians 2:7 asserts "That is the ages to come he might show the exceeding riches of His grace in His kindness toward us through Jesus Christ." In other words, more grace is coming.

There is an old story that I have shared often at funerals of believers as a reminder of the best is yet to come. Let me share it with you here:

> There was a woman who had been diagnosed with a terminal illness and had been given three months to live. As she was getting her things "in order," she contacted her pastor and had him come to her house to discuss certain aspects of her final wishes. She told him which songs she wanted sung at the service, what scriptures she would like read, and what outfit she wanted to be buried in. The woman also requested to be buried with her favorite Bible.
>
> Everything was in order and the pastor was preparing to leave when the woman suddenly remembered something very important to her.
>
> "There's one more thing," she said excitedly.
>
> "What's that?" came the pastor's reply.
>
> "This is very important," the woman continued. "I want to be buried with a fork in my right hand." The pastor stood looking at the woman, not knowing quite what to say. "That surprises you, doesn't it?" the woman asked.
>
> "Well, to be honest, I'm puzzled by the request," said the pastor.
>
> The woman explained, "In all my years of attending church socials and potluck dinners, I always remember that when the dishes of the main course were being cleared, someone would inevitably lean over and say, 'Keep your fork.' It was my favorite part because I knew that something better was coming . . . like velvety chocolate cake or deep-dish apple pie. Something wonderful, and with substance! So, I just want people to see me there in that casket with a fork in my hand and I want them to wonder 'What's with the fork?' Then I want you to tell them: 'Keep your fork. The best is yet to come.'"
>
> The pastor's eyes welled up with tears of joy as he hugged the woman good-bye. He knew this would be one of the last times he would see her before her death. But he also knew that the woman had a better grasp of heaven than he did. She *knew* that something better was coming.

At the funeral, people were walking by the woman's casket and they saw the pretty dress she was wearing and her favorite Bible and the fork placed in her right hand. Over and over the pastor heard the question "What's with the fork?" And over and over he smiled.

During his message, the pastor told the people of the conversation he had with the woman shortly before she died. He also told them about the fork and about what it symbolized to her. The pastor told the people how he could not stop thinking about the fork and told them that they probably would not be able to stop thinking about it either.

He was right.[2]

So the next time you reach down for your fork, let it remind you, oh so gently, that the best is yet to come.

First Peter 1:13 tells us what to do to prepare: "Wherefore gird up the loins of your mind, be sober, and hope to the end for the grace that is to be brought unto you and the revelation of Jesus Christ." And what is the source of all this? Grace.

Graced with Spiritual Blessings

Ephesians 1:3 makes it clear that we have been blessed "with all spiritual blessings in the Heavenlies." First Peter 2:4 states that "His divine power has given (graced us) all things that pertain to life and godliness." So, not only have we been graced regarding our sin, we also have been graced in many other ways.

Graced with Spiritual Gifts

The Greek language is such a precise language that it is not hard to understand why our Lord chose that language to pen the unsearchable riches of the New Testament. English translations, however, often miss the special nuances. The connection of grace and spiritual gifts is one such example. Without getting all "Greeky" on you, let me just say that the root word for grace and spiritual gifts is the same. The Greek word for grace transliterated

---

2. "Keep Your Fork." Accessed September 17, 2014. http://www.moytura.com/reflections/KeepYourFork.htm.

is *charis* and the word for spiritual gifts is *charisma*. Our spiritual gifts that we have are sourced to us out of his grace.

There are several passages in the New Testament that describe these spiritual gifts for us, particularly Rom 12 and 1 Cor 12–14. In these chapters there are several lists of what the believer has been graced with. The image is that of an actual body with head, arms, feet, etc. That picture is really a view of the body of Christ, with Jesus as the Head (Eph 1:22). The rest of the body (arms, legs, etc.) are made up of the believers whom God places as he so sees fit (1 Cor 12:18). God gifts (graces) us with a spiritual (grace) gift so we can have our place in the body and serve the Head as we minister to one another. And once again we see that this is an act of grace to us by God.

- Romans 12:3—"For I say through the grace given (graced) unto me, to every man that is among you, not to think of himself more highly than he ought to think, but to think soberly according as God has dealt to every man the measure of faith."
- Romans 12:4—"Having then gifts (root word – grace) differing according to the grace that is given to us."
- 1 Corinthians 12:14–18 (rather long section but so important here)— For the body is not one member, but many. If the foot shall say, "Because I am not the hand, I am not of the body"; is it therefore not of the body? And if the ear shall say, "Because I am not the eye, I am not of the body"; is it therefore not of the body? If the whole body *were* an eye, where *were* the hearing? If the whole *were* hearing, where *were* the smelling? But now hath God set the members every one of them in the body, as it hath pleased him. (Notice the emphasis on the foot, hand, ear, and eye (all graced in place by God). Again we are reminded that each grace gift has been placed there as God sees fit.)
- 1 Peter 4:10—"As every man has received the gift (grace), even so minister the same one to another, as good stewards of the manifold grace of God."

Grace has been extended to us in that we are given one or more grace gifts. We will develop this more later on in our discussion, but for now it should be clear that these gifts weren't given solely for our own benefit. Several times in these passages God specifies that we have been graced to grace others. First, we have been graced to minister for his glory (1 Pet 4:11), and second, for to minister to one another (1 Cor 12:7). Nowhere does the New

Testament teach that we have been gifted for our own personal benefit. Today, many churches teach personal gratification of spiritual gifts, which is simply contrary to grace and the Grace Bestower.

Everything we do and have in the body of Christ is simply because of God, and as a tribute to him, we should honor him for this grace bestowed upon us. We would not qualify to be graced were it not for his grace, and we would not have grace gifts, were it not for him, the Grace Gift Giver. If we are simply recipients of his grace, how can we glory in them for ourselves?

First Corinthians reminds us that if we are to glory, we are to glory in him. Our position in the body of Christ (a gift of grace), should cause us to give him praise and thanks, regardless of how lowly we believe it might be (1 Cor 1:26–31). Paul adds a great confirmation of this thought in 1 Cor 4:7: "For who makes thee to differ from another? And what have you that you have not received (grace gift)? Now if you did receive it, why do you glory, as if you had not received it?" One of the problems many believers have is that we think we are either deserving of these gifts or worthy in some manner. My friends, it is all about grace.

Graced with a Spiritual Body

Not only are we graced to be in a physical body to minister to one another, but we are also graced to be in this spiritual body (church) to be graced by those who are in the body with us. It works both ways. As we extend grace to others, grace returns to us. You cannot out-give God. Now we don't grace others to receive grace, but it happens because we are connected to a spiritual body.

Now before I explain this from 1 Corinthians, let me try to add some exhortations to those who may be reading and who have not truly connected to a local body (church). Far too many believers live as disconnected from the body. I often hear people say that they left the church, but have never left God. I beg to differ with that thought. Have you ever had a friend who you liked, but you did not necessarily care for his wife? Now how do you manage that? Do you just tell him that you want to be his friend, but want nothing to do with his bride? How do you think that will go? Now imagine telling that to Jesus. "I want to be with you, but can't stand your bride (the church)." Do you think he is fine with that? Additionally, you are cutting yourself off from regular church grace that comes from having a one-another relationship in the body. Maybe that is why Paul begins all his church writings with "grace to you."

Now how does this grace flesh itself out in the body? First, there is the harmony of the body. First Corinthians 12:12 teaches that the body is one with many members. We are able to make an amazing impact as we come together to form a body that mirrors him to a world that desperately needs to see his grace in action. But second, there is the grace that comes from each grace member to the other grace members. So, when one member suffers, all suffer. When one member rejoices, all the members rejoice (1 Cor 12:26). Now our physical body is so much the same. Have you ever had a small splinter in your finger that irritates your whole body? You can't focus on anything else till the splinter is removed. Yet, when it is removed, all the body rejoices and moves on. Our physical body is a picture of that spiritual body. And all our members are simply grace gifts to the body.

This is also important to remember when God sends people to your church or removes them. We need to recognize the sovereign hand of God in this process. I have seen over the years how this has come in all kinds of dimensions. People are transferred due to occupations and careers. Some are removed for sin. Some just need to move on. Then God brings another family to you that fills the gap. How does all this work? Well, I am convinced some of it is sinfulness on the part of humankind, but sometimes, God is setting the body up as he sees fit. A local church needs a hand, a foot, an ear. Who better than the Holy Spirit to direct the make-up of that body? We need to see people leaving as grace departures and those arriving as grace arrivals. What a fresh way to see the grace family!

Let me share a story with you from one of our church families that has recently gone through a lot of difficulties: loss of job, deaths, health issues. Listen to these words of encouragement:

Dear friends at MABC,

I wanted to thank everyone at MABC for the tremendous support that our family received during our difficult time over the last several months. During this time, I was laid off from work, had back surgery, and worst of all, my wife's dad passed away. But through it all, you supported us in so many ways. Many people gave us very generous gifts. Many people brought us delicious meals, which was a tremendous help to my wife while she was assisting her mother and father and taking care of myself after surgery. Others actually worked with her dad at the nursing home and took such great care of him. Some folks even brought groceries to our house. Others came to visit me while I was recovering at home. I know that many of you were praying for us and would call or email to see if we needed anything. Many were a blessing to my wife's mother by plowing the snow from her over 300-ft driveway.

Thank you all for your help, love, and support. We cannot thank you enough. You have all been a blessing to us and have demonstrated Christ's love. I hope that my family and I can be a blessing in return to our church family at MABC. My family and I are doing much better now, thanks be to God and to all of you. If anyone ever questions why it is important to be plugged into a local church, this is just one example—to love, support, serve, and care for one another. Thanks so much.

This is called the grace family in action. Members who have been graced understand that this grace has simply been given to them to grace others. This is the picture of the early church as well. Acts 2 describes this in detail for us as the early church practiced grace living by having all things in common, giving to every man as he had need, having favor with one another, and sharing on whatever level was necessary. Others were surprised at how much they loved one another. When the body practices grace living with one another, there is no limit to the impact for the kingdom.

Graced with Spiritual Communication with God

Far too many believers have forgotten that prayer is our privileged communication with God, and it is again all about grace. We only have access to him because of grace. Grace allows us to have an entrance right into the inner room of God. This access was all made possible when our Lord, dying on the cross, paid for our sins and propitiated us to the Father by his atoning work of grace. Matthew 27:51 reminds us of this truth as we see our Savior dying on the cross for our sins. During his agony, the veil in the temple was torn from top to bottom. This veil separated the Holy Place from the Holy of Holies. The temple had this veil as a reminder that only the high priest had access to God. All others must go through this high priest. God tore that veil himself (from top to bottom), and now we have access directly to God by his grace. We don't need anyone to go to God for us. The veil has been torn down.

The writer of Hebrews makes this point solidly for us: "Let us therefore, come boldly unto the throne of grace that we may obtain mercy and find grace in time of need" (Heb 4:16). The ability to come to the inner room (Holy of Holies) and pray is only made possible by his grace. That is why prayer is even called coming to the throne of grace.

Just think of all the people who live in this world. As of this writing, the number is more than 7.5 billion. How important is it to you to have an audience with God? Don't you think that the many who do not have this access would just love to have the chance? Living in America allows us so many wonderful freedoms that we take for granted. One in particular that is often overlooked is our free elections and right to vote. When an immigrant comes to our country from a nation that did not permit it, they rarely miss an opportunity to vote. Yet millions in America do not even bother. They take the great privilege for granted. I trust you will not allow yourself to miss out on the grace of voting, or the grace of prayer.

How many times have you heard a believer say, "I don't know how I would be able to go through what I do without the Lord." What they are implying, of course, is the value of prayer. We believers know the value of prayer and are so thankful that we have a God that neither slumbers nor sleeps. We can go to him anytime and for anything.

Now I can hear someone say, "Everyone has the privilege of prayer." In a generic sense, that is correct. But God is not bound to respond to the prayers of those who are not his children (Ps 66:18). Just as if we had our kids on a playground with other community kids and one of the other children fell and scratched her knee, we might be moved with compassion, but our care would be limited because the girl is not our child. God delights in the prayers of his children. He runs to you when you pray, so cry out to him!

Graced with Scripture

People like to argue that the Bible is available to most of the world. Yet 1 Cor 2:14 makes it clear that they may read the Bible, but it is foolishness to them. The Bible is only spiritually discerned by those who are graced to have a relationship with the Author. As a matter of fact, the Bible is the only book that in order to understand the book, you have to have a personal relationship with the Author. Believers have that grace.

Understanding How We Have Been Graced Spiritually

On several occasions in Scripture, the Word and grace are even intertwined in such a way to further demonstrate this point.

- John 1:14—"And the Word was made flesh and dwelt among us and we beheld His glory, the glory of the only Begotten of the Father, full of grace and truth."
- Acts 13:43—"Paul and Barnabas were persuaded to continue in the grace of God."
- Acts 13:44—"And the next Sabbath day came almost the whole city together to hear the Word of God." (That is what "continuing in grace" in 13:43 means.)
- Acts 20:32—"And now brethren, I commend you to God and to the Word of His Grace."
- Colossians 3:16—"Let the Word of Christ dwell in you richly, in all wisdom teaching and admonishing one another in Psalms and hymns and spiritual songs, singing with grace in your hearts to the Lord."

When we hold in our hands the Word of God, when we hear the Word of God, when we memorize the Word of God, it is grace that permits us to understand and grasp the truths of grace. We are unlike the Ethiopian eunuch who had to have the Word explained to him (Acts 8) because we are graced with an understanding that truly allows the Word to be a lamp unto our feet and a light unto our path.

Graced with the Holy Spirit

There is little need to develop this thought beyond just a few statements. If it is grace that allows us the privilege of being a child of God, then the gift of the Holy Spirit can only be seen as a grace gift. Second Corinthians 13:14 connects the Holy Spirit and grace together, but it is Heb 10:29 whereby he is called the Spirit of Grace. The Holy Spirit is the one who develops our grace walk on this side of eternity.

- We are saved by grace – work of the Holy Spirit
- We walk this journey by grace – enabled by the Holy Spirit
- We pray only by the enabling of the Holy Spirit
- We understand the Word by the discernment of the Holy Spirit

Our whole Christian journey is one by which the Holy Spirit enables us to take the journey one step at a time for his glory. This enablement is simply the grace of God in action. As a result we need to be cautious not to grieve or quench the Holy Spirit, who is our down payment of great things to come.

Graced with a New Description

We have been put in the witness protection program and have been given a new name, new identity, new location, and a new vision in life. The difference in the government's program and God's is that we need to talk about our past so people can see just what God has done for us.

Before I met Christ, I was incomplete and undone. Now in Christ I have a new identity. This is true of all who have come to know Jesus as their Savior. We have become a new creation in Christ. Old things are passed away (old identity), and now we are new in him.

Look at this list and let these become a statement of God's grace to you:

I am Accepted in Christ

John 1:12	I am God's child.
John 15:15	I am Christ's friend.
Romans 5:1	I have been justified.
1 Corinthians 6:17	I am united with the Lord and one with him in spirit.
1 Corinthians 6:20	I have been bought with a price, I belong to God.
1 Corinthians 12:27	I am a member of Christ's body.
Ephesians 1:1	I am a saint.
Ephesians 1:5	I have been adopted as God's child.
Ephesians 2:18	I have direct access to God through the Holy Spirit.
Colossians 1:14	I have been redeemed and forgiven of all my sins.
Colossians 2:10	I am complete in Christ.

Understanding How We Have Been Graced Spiritually

I am Secure in Christ

Romans 8:1-2	I am free forever from condemnation.
Romans 8:28	I am assured that all things work together for good.
Romans 8:33–34	I am free from any condemning charges against me.
Romans 8:35	I cannot be separated from the love of God.
2 Corinthians 1:21	I have been established anointed and sealed by God.
Colossians 3:3	I am hidden with Christ in God.
Philippians 1:6	I am confident that the good work God has begun in me will be perfected.
Philippians 3:20	I am a citizen of heaven.
2 Timothy 1:7	I have not been given a spirit of fear but of power love and a sound mind.
Hebrews 4:16	I can find grace and mercy in time of need.
1 John 5:18	I am born of God and the evil one cannot touch me.

I Am Significant in Christ

Matthew 5:13-14	I am the salt and light of the earth.
John 15:1,5	I am a branch of the true vine, a channel of his life.
John 15:16	I have been chosen and appointed to bear fruit.
Acts 1:8	I am a personal witness of Christ's.
1 Corinthians 3:16	I am God's temple.
2 Corinthians 5:17-20	I am a minister of reconciliation.
2 Corinthians 6:1	I am God's co-worker.
Ephesians 2:6	I am seated with Christ in the heavenly realm.

Ephesians 2:10	I am God's workmanship.
Ephesians 3:12	I may approach God with freedom and confidence.
Philippians 4:13	I can do all things through Christ who strengthens me.[11]

Just let the above truths sink in, and couple the thought with the reality that under no circumstances are you in any way deserving of even one of these. All of these changes are grace extended to people who are most undeserving. With these great truths we find our answers to all the important questions of life.

"Why am I here?" You are here because a loving God so cared to invest into you that you were put here for this God to display his love to you and make you a conduit of his grace to others. Are others being graced by God through you?

"What was I made for?" You are here to display that grace God invested in you to the world. God does not make any mistakes, nor does he make any junk. We live today in a throw-away society. We no longer fix washers, dryers, or electronics (especially if they are getting older). Instead, we just discard and get the newer model. We throw away unwanted children under the protection of the government called abortion. We put our older family members in homes because we don't want to be bothered with them (Of course, there are cases where a home is necessary, yet I have visited many of these homes and find very capable senior adults just put there for convenience.) We have simply lost a true theology that sees a sovereign God who makes all things work perfectly according to the counsel of his will.

This same kind of theology slips into the believing community. As a result, many of God's children are walking around paralyzed and unfruitful for his kingdom. They are stuck in the grip of Satan, who has them captive by false views of themselves, called by all sorts of humanistic names. We need to see ourselves through the eyes of God and not through the eyes of secular humanity. We are children of God, graced beyond our wildest imaginations. And when we begin to live out our lives in light of how he sees us and how he has graced us, our potential is limitless. Instead, we often live in the bondage of the enemy, surrounded by the crippling views that cause us to focus on what we are not, instead of focusing on who we are.

---

3. Neil T Anderson. *Living Free in Christ*. Ventura, Calif., U.S.A.: Regal Books, 1993.

Understanding How We Have Been Graced Spiritually

I heard a story about a study years ago where a group of teachers were called together from a particular school and told that they were going to be rewarded for being the best teachers in the school. First, they were not to tell anyone of the experiment. If they did, they would be removed from the program. Second, they were going to be given the top students in the school. The goal was simple; they were to see just how far they could take these students academically in one year. The students were tested as they entered the program and would be tested at the end. When the year concluded, the students were tested as scheduled, and the results were amazing. Each student had achieved incredible results and the entire group was called in to hear the program director's explanation. In front of the group, she went on to commend the teachers and students for this incredible advancement. Each needed to see what great strides they had made, both teachers and students. The director then went on to explain that two things needed to be corrected. First, the teachers that were selected were not the top teachers in the school. Second, neither were the students. They had actually picked teachers and students who were performing on an average level. The purpose of the program was to see if it made any difference that these teachers and students felt like someone believed in them.

Our story is similar in many ways. We too have been selected for a program. We too have been given a chance to make a major difference. We too have been given a list of credentials that make us the best of the world. We will realize that we truly accomplished what we did simply because of grace, not our own gifts. I often compare myself to the boy with the bag lunch that came to Jesus to offer his meal for the feeding of the multitude. The only difference between me and that boy is that by the time I have brought my lunch to Jesus, my bag is torn, and the ingredients are gone. I bring to Jesus my empty bag, and he gives me a new bag full of all that he desires me to have. I then can leave his presence with the capability of feeding the multitudes. God's children need to stop seeing themselves simply as clay pots and empty bags. We are in Christ. And that makes us graced and very capable of gracing others.

CHAPTER 3

Understanding How We Have Been Graced Temporally

Personal Grace

Grace isn't always apparent to us. God doesn't come up to us, smack us in the nose, and say "See! I'm giving you grace right now while you're stuck in traffic!" Yet that is often precisely what he is doing. Many times in this earthly, temporal world, we are graced without even being aware of it—until later. As you read this chapter, pray that you will see your circumstances, no matter how difficult, as grace events. It will give you an entirely new perspective.

Grace in an Accident or Tragedy

It is often hard for people who have been beaten down, discouraged, and ill focused to truly see grace in all its dimensions. We are prone to only see major grace events, while often the daily grace happenings are overlooked. How many times have you traveled many miles for a vacation, wedding, family event, or whatever, and arrived safely and never thought much about the protection God has just provided for you? As I stated previously, it only takes one car accident to bring us back to reality. If the Lord guided you through that accident with minimal damage, then the vision of grace seems clearer. Yet how many do we never see and just miss the grace event, like

Understanding How We Have Been Graced Temporally

the time where you had a flat tire and were late for something, or the time a child had to go "potty" and you begrudgingly pulled over to a rest stop, or the time a family member delayed you. How many times were these divine interventions of grace?

Just look at this list of those who missed the terrorist attacks of 9/11:[1]

- Lorraine Wallace relates that everyone in her office was late that morning, which was highly unusual because her boss was a stickler for punctuality. Busses and trains were late, people were out sick, etc. Only one person was in the office on time, and that person got out safely. (*The Times-Reporter*, Ohio)
- Debbie Archimbaud was frustrated because of a late bus and lack of time for breakfast, making her ten minutes late for work. (*The Pocono Record*, Pennsylvania)
- Rob Herzog had been frustrated with a late plane, unusual train stops, and the train door slamming in his face just as he made his way through the crowd. (*The Tampa Tribune*, Florida)

From their perspective that morning, these people (and many more) only realized that they were running late. They relate how frustrated they were as they tried to get to work on time. But they didn't see what God saw that day.

Grace isn't only found in the things that don't happen to us or the near misses. Grace is also in the painful things we do experience. One such example would be the story of Mike Donehey, the lead singer for Tenth Avenue North. You can hear his full story on YouTube, but let me offer the condensed version. In high school he was a good athlete with great potential, but on his way to a soccer game, he was in a serious car accident. His back was broken, and his future career—indeed his ability to play any sport—was ended. Where was God? Where was the grace? God began showing him right away:

1. For a long time his life was in danger, but he lived.
2. Doctors were in doubt that he would ever walk again, but he can walk.
3. As he lay on his bed for weeks, he was given a guitar. He had never played guitar but it gave him something to do. What evolved from that is the popular Christian music group Tenth Avenue North. Had

---

1. "They Were Late for Work on 9/11." September 11, 2006. Accessed September 2, 2014. <http://september-11.blogspot.com/feeds/posts/default?orderby=updated>

he never been in that accident, he may never have given his life to full-time Christian ministry. His song, "Worn," is a testimony of this story.

Donehey saw (and continues to see) evidence of God's grace in an accident that was, from a human perspective, completely devastating. And those evidences of God's grace continue to mount in all situations as our eyes open to see how he is working.

Grace in Losing a Job

I hesitate to use a personal story in this book, but this example is so real and vivid that the Lord pressed me to do so. While finishing my Master of Divinity degree, I was teaching in a Bible college. The academic dean had already informed me that he was grooming me to be a full-time teacher at the college. I had not personally envisioned that, but I was open to whatever the Lord preferred. I had been bought with a price, so who was I to argue with my God? In the summer prior to my last year of study, the dean called me at my home and informed me that the incoming president had decided that all part-time staff needed to be cut, and that included me. It was quite a surprise; I had been assigned to teach three different classes in the fall! I was newly married with seminary bills and all living expenses, and now I had no job. Anger and bitterness began to creep in.

However, I didn't have time to harbor them much, because I was searching for some kind of employment so I could finish my final year of graduate school. God graciously provided a youth ministry in an inner-city church where we saw a number of kids come to faith in Christ. That alone was worth being laid off, but there was more to come. As I was nearing the end of the year, a friend told me of a church that was looking for a pastor. I had sensed God was moving me in that direction, but had no clear confirmation of that leading. Stepping out in faith, I applied for the position, and have now been pastor of that same church for nearly 30 years. God's grace allowed me to get fired. If I had stayed on that college campus, I may have gone into teaching and never sought out church ministry.

God's grace gifts may not look like gifts at the time, but they can prevent us from doing something in the wrong direction or lead us to something that is firmly in his will. Could I have been graced to stay and teach at college? Of course, but after almost 30 years of pastoral ministry, I can see that is exactly how I was wired by God. It took the grace gift of being fired to lead me to where God wanted me to be. If I had stayed mired in the circumstances, I might have missed the gift entirely. And there are probably many more that I don't recognize!

Grace in a Health Crisis

Most of us evaluate grace in health as being completely healthy from all views of the body. Expectant parents often say something like, "As long as the baby is healthy, that is all we care about." Then, when the baby is born healthy and without defects, we conclude we have been graced. But what is a healthy baby? Who defines that a healthy baby really is? Are we concluding that a baby born with differences is really not a grace gift? Spending some time with some of these families quickly dispels that notion! How special it is to hear families talk about their child with differences as one of the greatest gifts God has ever graced them with. God's grace comes designed very differently from our expectations!

Even tragic accidents that turn out very differently from Mike Donehey's can be grace gifts. Just ask Joni Erikson Tada what she has discovered from the grace event of being paralyzed as a teen in a swimming accident. Was this a grace gift? She has personally ministered to thousands of people in her journey as a quadriplegic. God has used her greatly to help many that are unable to speak and lead for themselves. Thank God for gracing the Christian community with this wonderful woman of faith! Again, God's grace gifts come in all shapes and sizes.

Grace in Death

As a pastor, I have traveled many paths with believers who have watched loved ones pass in death. Death is no respecter of persons. It comes to all ages, races, genders, and social and political hierarchies.

But should all deaths be viewed with horror and despair? I remember getting a call when a family of six was in a tragic accident and four of them were killed. I have been called when a small child died a mysterious death. I walked on the porch one day to console a wife whose husband was tragically killed in an accident. I am not for one moment going to try to explain these events, nor try to suggest that there is not real earthly pain involved. Death has a great amount of pain associated with it, and I would never want to minimize or make light of this pain. But still there is grace in this.

There is a fable that tells about two angels who were on a journey. They stopped to spend the night in the home of a wealthy family. The family was rude and refused to let the angels stay in the mansion's guest room. Instead, the angels were given a small space in the cold basement. As they made their bed on the hard floor, the older angel saw a hole in the wall and repaired it.

When the younger angel asked why, the older angel replied, "Things aren't always what they seem."

The next night the pair came to rest at the house of a very poor, but very hospitable farmer and his wife. After sharing what little food they had, the couple let the angels sleep in their bed where they could have a good night's rest.

When the sun came up the next morning the angels found the farmer and his wife in tears. Their only cow, whose milk had been their sole income, lay dead in the field.

The younger angel was infuriated and asked the older angel, "How could you have let this happen? The first man had everything, yet you helped him. The second family had little but was willing to share everything, and you let the cow die."

"Things aren't always what they seem," the older angel replied. "When we stayed in the basement of the mansion, I noticed there was gold stored in that hole in the wall. Since the owner was so obsessed with greed and unwilling to share his good fortune, I sealed the wall so he wouldn't find it.

"Then last night as we slept in the farmer's bed, the angel of death came for his wife. I gave him the cow instead. Things aren't always what they seem."[2]

Sometimes that is exactly what happens when things don't turn out the way they should. If you have faith, you need to trust that the outcome has a purpose. You just might not know it until sometime later.

In order to properly understand grace in death, we have to see through his eyes and not earthly eyes. Since we are limited, that is hard for us to do, but there are worst things in life than death. You have also heard of dying grace. It is that grace God gives to people hurting through a death. Death is real, but God will not permit you to suffer it alone. The Bible reassures us, "Yea though I walk through the valley of the shadow of death, I will fear no evil, for you are with me" (Ps 23:4, NKJV).

---

2. "Two Traveling Angels Story for All Scouts." Accessed October 1, 2014. http://www.boyscouttrail.com/content/story/two_traveling_angels-196.asp.

Understanding How We Have Been Graced Temporally

- I wonder how many times has God taken someone home "early" because they were about to ruin the testimony that they had spent years building? Would that be grace?
- I wonder how many times God has taken someone home "early" because they had finished what he had given them to do. Would that be grace?
- I wonder how many times God has taken someone home "early" because there are earthly lessons to be learned in suffering. Would that be grace?
- I wonder how many times God has taken someone home "early" because he has reasons that only eternity will reveal? Would that be grace?

Our years are numbered by the Lord, and because he is a sovereign God, he has every day of our lives in his hands. When he takes a person home, it is not our right to suggest that it was premature. When God is ready for a saint to come home, it will always be on his timetable. And you can be sure that there is grace in the event as well as grace for us who are left behind to journey.

My younger brother's wife passed on about four years ago due to a brain tumor. Our family journeyed with him and his family during that season. This year he spoke at our men's retreat and shared a depth of suffering and sanctification that I am convinced can only come when a child of God faces such a challenge. Was it easy? Absolutely not. Was it my brother's choice? Absolutely not. Was there grace available? Absolutely. Death has its own way of releasing that God controlled grace at the right time when needed.

Many believers have heard the story of the five missionaries who were killed in Ecuador in 1956. When the news hit the air waves, the mourning, the doubting, the questioning circled as smoke around a fire. Did any of this make sense? Five aspiring missionaries with families, potential, and great passion were taken in the prime of their lives. How was this grace in action? You can read this story in Elizabeth Elliot's book, *Through Gates of Splendor*. Through the deaths of these men, the tribesmen began to listen, and their hearts began to open. Her husband, Jim Elliot, one of the men who was killed, had written, "He is no fool who gives what he cannot keep to gain what he cannot lose." That is grace at its purest form.

Graced 2 Grace

Grace in an Affliction

Even earthly struggles of a more mundane nature can be grace gifts. The Psalmist makes this point extremely clear when he says, "Before I was afflicted, I went astray: but now I have kept thy word" (Ps 119:67, 71). There is no question that many saints have experienced that through earthly struggles. But how often have we seen these as grace gifts?

For the most part, we see someone who is beautiful by earthly standards and we conclude that he or she is blessed (graced). We see someone gifted in sports, work, abilities, or some earthly capability and feel that that person has been especially blessed. We may even wish we had their looks, abilities, or some other attribute. But might not our "defects" be just as much a gift of grace as their supposed blessings? In point of fact, how often do their blessings bring about challenges that those who never have had those blessings ever experience? Esther is a great example. She was very beautiful and probably widely envied, but her very beauty put her in a serious situation. We see how God used the challenge that began with her beauty to benefit his people. But at the time, those who weren't as beautiful didn't face her challenges and may even have envied her for the "easy" life she had.

What kind of a life do movie stars, sports figures, politicians, etc. really have? We look at the glamour of their blessed positions, but do we really want to be accosted hourly by photographers trying to pick up juicy photos while people are constantly asking for our autograph or a picture? We have all read about celebrities who have said that they miss being normal. Who really is the graced individual?

So if an affliction or disease or limitation robs us of the "easy" life such as celebrities might have, might that affliction actually be an act of grace? Or on another note, how many of us have really looked back upon an affliction and have seen the hand of God within it? I know personally that when I have been tried through the deep waters of affliction, I have learned more incredible truths of God.

G.D. Watson (1845-1924) a Wesleyan Methodist pastor, saw a huge amount of suffering in his time. Yet he writes triumphantly in "The Vestibule of Heaven":

> If God has called you to be really like Jesus in your spirit, he will draw you into a life of crucifixion and humility, and put on you such demands of obedience that he will not allow you to follow other Christians; and in many ways he will seem to let other good people do things that he will not let you do. Other Christians and

ministers who seem very religious and useful may push themselves, pull wires and work schemes to carry out their schemes, but you cannot do it; and if you attempt it, you will meet with such failure and rebuke from the Lord as to make you sorely penitent. Others may brag on themselves, on their work, on their success, on their writings, but the Holy Spirit will not allow you to do any such thing; and if you begin it, he will lead you into some deep mortification that will make you despise yourself and all your good works.

Others may be allowed to succeed in making money, but it is likely that God will keep you poor, because he wants you to have something far better than gold, and that is helpless dependence upon him, that he may have the privilege (the right) of supplying your needs day by day out of an unseen treasury. The Lord will let others be honoured and put forward, and keep you hidden away in obscurity, because he wants some choice fragrant fruit for his coming glory which can only be produced in the shade. He will let others do a work for him and get the credit for it, but he will let you work and toil on without knowing how much you are doing; and then to make your work still more precious, he will let others get the credit for the work you have done, and this will make your reward ten times greater when Jesus comes.

The Holy Spirit will put a watch over you, with a jealous love, and will rebuke you for little words and feelings or for wasting your time, over which other Christians never seem distressed. So make up your mind that God is an infinite Sovereign, and has the right to do as he pleases with his own, and he may not explain to you a thousand things which may puzzle your reason in his dealings with you. He will take you at your word and if you absolutely sell yourself to be his slave, he will wrap you up in a jealous love and let other people say and do many things which he will not let you say or do.

Settle it forever that you are to deal directly with the Holy Spirit, and that he is to have the privilege of tying your tongue, or chaining your hand, or closing your eyes, in ways that he does not deal with others. Now when you are so possessed with the Living God, that you are in your secret heart pleased and delighted over the peculiar, personal, private, jealous guardianship of the Holy Spirit over your life, you will have found the vestibule of heaven.

This reasoning is exemplified in the Apostle Paul, who was given a thorn in the flesh (some level of affliction). Regardless of what the "thorn" may have been, we notice Paul's conclusion: God's grace was made perfect in

Paul's weakness (2 Cor 12:9). In the next verse he adds that he is thankful for such affliction. Physical afflictions cause us to dive to a depth that would otherwise be unreachable.

Please remember that God has never allowed or caused anything into our lives that is not ultimately for our good and his glory. Don't foster bitterness at the outward circumstances and miss the grace gifts. May we learn to say with Joseph, "What you [his brothers] meant for evil, God intended for good" (Gen 50:20). He wants us better, not bitter.

Summary Thoughts

We have seen just a small sampling of the grace acts that don't look very grace-full when viewed through human eyes. We are so limited in our ability to see that we need to draw close to him daily so that we may be aware of his grace acts in our lives in whatever form they appear. His grace is a continual flow that is being poured out on us without any interruption. We miss it because we attempt to decipher events based on how we feel or how they appear. When we submit to God's timetable and allow him to prove himself we then see that all the events that trouble us have as their source God's grace.

United States Grace

The predominant audience reading this book will probably be Americans. So, if you are not from the U.S., this section may not be as relevant to you. However, it would be difficult to talk about being blessed without talking about one of the most materially blessed nations in the world, the United States of America.

I doubt anyone would attempt to question that statement. Even "America the Beautiful," a popular patriotic chorus, says, "America, America, God shed his grace on thee." That is both a prayer and a statement, especially as the song points out numerous evidences of this blessing. Just think, this country has been:

- blessed with prosperity.
- blessed with military strength.
- blessed with a vital culture.

Understanding How We Have Been Graced Temporally

- blessed with health.
- blessed with leisure activities.
- blessed with safety.

We could just keep going. From shore to shore and from boundary to boundary, we could list blessings. Obviously, our country has many faults and many problems. We are not perfect, but yet tens of thousands of people want to come here, even illegally, because we have been greatly blessed.

In my travels I have had to get many shots to avoid the diseases of the countries I visit. I have been warned to drink only water that comes from a bottle that I personally open. I have been cautioned to eat only fruit, vegetables, and salads that I have personally washed in water from the bottle I opened. I remember one trip when I got off the plane and was heading through customs, I saw a sign that read "Welcome Home." What a thought. Unless you travel outside the U.S., you may not see just how graced you are to live in this great country. But can so obvious a blessing actually become a curse?

Warning about United States Grace

We recently had a missionary from China come to our church and discuss the evangelistic outreach in China. He brought to us an interesting truth that I had never heard explained before. He talked about the missionary advances in the last 30 years or so under communist oppression. The underground church is flourishing in spite of continual increase in persecution and opposition. Now, he explained, China is experiencing a different kind of struggle than ever before. It is the struggle of being materially blessed. The country is beginning to experience economic world-wide prestige. Remember when "made in China" meant junk to be avoided? Now the country is emerging as an economic world power, and has already surpassed the U.S. Yet with this economic development comes a materialistic mindset. The missionary said that the Chinese want to emulate us. Their material prosperity makes them complacent, and the missionaries are discovering how difficult it is to evangelize when people are comfortable right where they are. Is this grace really grace at all?

Now let's go back and consider America's journey of the same kind. Statistics continue to prove that in our country, when we feel we have been most blessed and when we are most comfortable, we have been the least open to God and his teachings. The blessings of God have consistently caused Americans to drift from him and to be "self" sufficient. Just think about your own journey. Have you drawn closer to God in times of material blessing or in times of troubles? Today, evangelism in our country is much harder due to economic progress. Although many are struggling now, we still have much material advantage over the world.

When terrorists attacked our country in 2001, there was a sense of people crying out to God that I had not seen for some time. We were vulnerable, exposed, and hurting as a nation. You could even see bi-partisan agreement in the nation's capital. Churches saw an increase in attendance as people called to the God that they had abandoned. Of course as the pain wore off (I realize that many still carry the pain but the majority of Americans have gone on as if it never happened), God was once again put on the back burner. It demonstrates that we seem to thirst for God only when the water supply is low. So have the blessings of America really become a curse?

With the seeming materialistic blessing also comes the curse of hoarding. It seems the more one has, the less benevolent he or she is. Although there are some rich people who have been greatly generous in their sharing, for the most part the giving community is not the rich. Those with the most tend to hoard and keep for themselves. The most blessed become the stingiest. It appears that the blessings steal our hearts (Matt 6:21) so we become controlled by the blessings rather than controlled by the "Blesser."

Scripture discusses the danger of the cares of life choking out God (Matt 13:22) and his ultimate priority over us. We become squeezed into the mold of the world (Rom 12:1–2) and don't even notice it. It usually is gradual and subtle. We have more and need more to keep the more we have so we are working more. Did you get that?

I remember hearing the old saying that some people are "so heavenly minded that they are no earthly good." What that suggests is that there are some people who are so into Heaven that they are living on a different plane and unable to relate to this world and make a difference. Honestly, this problem is pretty rare, if not entirely nonexistent. Instead, what we have is a generation of people who have so immersed themselves into this world that they are no heavenly good. The materialism that has so drawn our hearts has caused us to fall in love with this world, and we have forgotten that to do so makes us an enemy of God (1 John 2:15–17). Our treasures are being laid up on the earth and are stealing our hearts. These are all concerns that our Savior pointed out to us when he was on the earth. How can we call ourselves followers of Jesus Christ who lived a life separate from the world, when we are immersing ourselves in the world?

Over the years, God has blessed me with the privilege of visiting several countries and to see poverty in ways that have caused me to shudder. I have seen houses that few of us would even enter, let alone abide in. I have seen meat thick with flies in the market. I have also had the privilege to be in some of the homes of the people who live in these countries. The conclusion that I have come to accept is that the more a believer has on the earth in material blessings, the less he has a heart after God. (This is a generalization, because I have found believers on both ends of the spectrum. I have seen self-centered impoverished and rich benevolent and vice versa.) In general, the believers who seem by the world's standards to have been graced or blessed the least seem to have the greatest joy. It is almost as if they have nothing but Jesus. Maybe they are the most graced after all?

World Grace

It is possible after a section like our previous one that someone could conclude that nations that are not like America have not been physically blessed at all, and it might be an argument worth making. Yet as the last section explained, physical blessing may be a judgment in disguise.

John MacArthur, in his book entitled *The Love of God*, devotes an entire chapter to "The Love of God for Humanity." He argues that although God loves the entire world that does not mean the entire world is going to Heaven. He also has a section in that chapter about common grace: "Common grace is a term theologians use to describe the goodness of God to all mankind universally." He describes it as the "love and goodness of God," which is simply his grace to mankind. Here it is in its entirety:

> If you question the love and goodness of God to all, look again at the world in which we live. Someone might say, "There's a lot of sorrow in the world." The only reason the sorrow and tragedy stand out is because there is also much joy and gladness. The only reason we recognize the ugliness is that God has given us so much beauty. The only reason we feel the disappointment is that there is so much that satisfies.[3]

---

3. MacArthur, John. *The Love of God.* (Dallas: Word, 1996), 117.

I could not agree more. There is much to say about the common grace that exists in every human situation. You may perhaps want to argue that in some situations, common grace can't exist. In a world with much evil as we have, there are some stories that are truly unimaginable. To the contrary, common grace does exist universally and it can be found in every community as a whole. It also would be worth adding that God has written himself on the heart of every man. That alone is grace.

So how is this grace universal? This list details some things that can be found world-wide, in every country, if not every day.

- Joy and happiness
- Health – although there are diseases, not all are unhealthy all the time
- Family
- Success
- Taste, touch, feel, see, hear
- Cool breezes
- Warm, sunny days
- Smells and aromas
- Laughter, stories, and memories
- And the fact of the existence of God himself (Ps 19)

These universal examples of grace seem so small in comparison to American material grace, but for people in many countries, these are all they have and they don't know the difference. It is hard to know the joys of what you don't have, especially if you don't even know these joys exist.

Often Overlooked Benefits of Grace

Living in America puts me at a disadvantage in discussing this next section, but it is absolutely necessary to get the complete picture. Although I have visited many countries, I certainly would not consider myself an authority. But what I have observed seems to be rather consistent with discussing world grace and how the people live in the circumstances that they do. Let me try to explain.

Paul makes an incredible statement in 1 Tim 6:7–8: "For we brought nothing into this world, and it is certain we can carry nothing out. And having food and raiment let us be therewith content." How many people do you know would be content with just food and clothing? In America, I am not sure I have found anyone who would say that if those were all that they had, they would be content. Yet I can say that in other countries, there are those that have only food and clothing, and yet seem more content than those who have much more. And to add to that, their clothing was often not something you or I would have, and their food was basic, and often very little.

So, how do these people have contentment? They have learned that since they only have food and clothing, they must be content with their Lord and Savior on a deeper level than many ever understand. What if we had only food or clothing? Would it make us bitter, or would it cause us to fall at the feet of our Savior? It appears that many who are without choose to fall at the feet of God and rely daily upon him for food, shelter, protection, and daily care. They have no credit cards, no savings, no extras, and in a real sense, all they have is the Lord to fall upon. I am certainly not saying that we all need to be in that kind of condition, but would it really be all that bad?

How often does Scripture teach us as followers to be diligent and to set our affection on things above, not on the earth? We are told to not love this world or the things that are in this world. We are told that this world is not our home; we are just strangers and pilgrims. Yet how many of us are consumed by the things that are in the world? Even the godliest American family struggles with balancing the Kingdom call and building their own kingdom.

Just think of the American pressures and obsessions that control our time that are not significant to most of the world.

- The hours spent on our lawns and gardens (excluding food).
- The hours spent with sports
- The hours spent on house work
- The hours spent on leisure events like movies, television, etc.
- The hours spent on travel, hobbies, hunting, fishing

My point is world grace—the grace of having little—may be more grace than we think. If we are not consumed with the above list, how much more time would we have to be immersed in Jesus? Do all the people that don't have these distractions immerse themselves in Jesus? Of course not, but what I am saying is that the world can so consume our hearts that our devotion might not be committed as it is for those who have only Jesus.

The Need for Grace Recipients

Jesus made a profound statement about the poor when he said "You will always have the poor with you" (Matt 26:11). Now what exactly does that mean? Well, for one thing, no matter how devoted we may be to stop world hunger and poverty, it is clear from Jesus' own prophetic words that it is not going to happen. That does not mean we should not try, just as the knowledge that all men are not going to be saved does not mean we don't make an effort to win all for Christ. But there is something else profound about what Jesus said here; namely, we are going to always have the poor *with us*. What that means is there will always be folks that need someone to share with them, help them, serve them, care for them, give to them, and assist. If all nations and peoples have equal materialistic grace, who would we share with? God has set up an amazing program right in front of our eyes.

God graces some people to be givers of grace and God graces others to be recipients of grace. Remember the words of our Savior on this when he said, "It is more blessed to give than to receive" (Acts 20:35). Probably all of us have been on both sides of this grace. We have had the amazing privilege to share grace with others and we have had the humbling experience of being in need of the grace from others. Look at the needs in the world:

- 852 million people across the world are hungry, up from 842 million a year ago.
- Every day, more than 16,000 children die from hunger-related causes—one child every five seconds.[4]

In essence, hunger is the most extreme form of poverty, where individuals or families cannot afford to meet their most basic need for food.

Hunger manifests itself in many ways other than starvation and famine. Most poor people who battle hunger deal with chronic undernourishment and vitamin or mineral deficiencies, which result in stunted growth, weakness, and heightened susceptibility to illness.

---

4. "MillionsOfMouths.com—Website about Global Poverty and Hunger." MillionsOfMouths.com. Accessed October 1, 2014.

Countries in which a large portion of the population battles hunger daily are usually poor and often lack the social safety nets we enjoy, such as soup kitchens, food stamps, and job training programs. When a family that lives in a poor country cannot grow enough food or earn enough money to buy food, there is nowhere to turn for help.

Facts and Figures on International Hunger and Poverty:[5]

- In the developing world, more than 1.2 billion people currently live below the international poverty line, earning less than $1 per day.
- Among this group of poor people, many have problems obtaining adequate, nutritious food for themselves and their families. As a result, 815 million people in the developing world are undernourished. They consume less than the minimum amount of calories essential for sound health and growth.
- Undernourishment negatively affects people's health, productivity, sense of hope and overall well-being. A lack of food can stunt growth, slow thinking, sap energy, hinder fetal development and contribute to mental retardation.
- Economically, the constant securing of food consumes valuable time and energy of poor people, allowing less time for work and earning income.
- Socially, the lack of food erodes relationships and feeds shame so that those most in need of support are often least able to call on it.

Go to the World Food Programme website and click on either "Counting the Hungry" or "Interactive Hunger Map" for presentations on hunger and poverty around the world.

The United States isn't left out of this count. Look at statistics that affect our communities:

- 38.2 million people—including 14 million children—live in households that experience hunger or the risk of hunger. This represents more than one in ten households in the United States (11.9 percent). This is an increase of 1.9 million, from 36.3, million in 2003.

---

5. "World Hunger Facts." Good Works Walk. Accessed September 2, 2014. http://www.goodworkswalk.net/world-hunger-facts/.

- 3.9 percent of U.S. households experience hunger. Some people in these households frequently skip meals or eat too little, sometimes going without food for a whole day. 10.7 million people, including 3 million children, live in these homes.

- 8.0 percent of U.S. households are at risk of hunger. Members of these households have lower quality diets or must resort to seeking emergency food because they cannot always afford the food they need. 27.5 million people, including 10.6 million children, live in these homes.

- Research shows that preschool and school-aged children who experience severe hunger have higher levels of chronic illness, anxiety and depression, and behavior problems than children with no hunger.[6]

But what is often overlooked is that God has blessed nations such as ours with the ability to make a great impact on these needs. We get to be the sharer of the grace that God has bestowed upon us. As we give, they who have been graced to be in a position of absolute trust in him alone, get to see God move the hearts of people to be his hands and feet. Jesus made that clear when he said that as we feed the poor, we have actually fed him (Matt. 25:35). Now this is not some kind of share the wealth and communistic thinking. It is actually the way the first-century church operated if we care to examine Acts 2:41–47. Notice what happened in the early church.

- Acts 2:44—"And all that believed were together and had all things common."

- Acts 2:45—"And sold their possessions and goods, and parted them to all men, as every man had need."

- Acts 2:47—"And the Lord added daily to the number being saved." (NKJV)

The early church grew and spread quickly. At Pentecost, there were people from many nations represented, all of whom heard the Word and then took it with them back to their country (Acts 2:11). Later on in Acts the church shares with other needy people outside of Jerusalem (Acts 11:27–30). There are basically two kinds of believers—those who have been graced materially to have and those who have been grace to have not. We can learn from both of these peoples, as both have grace to share.

---

6. "Hunger and Poverty Fact Sheet." Feeding America. Accessed November 5, 2014.

Understanding How We Have Been Graced Temporally

I will spend more time on the specifics of how this is to be accomplished later in the book, but for now, let's remind ourselves that God graces us all differently, and we need to determine what we are to do with the grace bestowed to each of us. One thing is for sure; grace that does not flow out from us will cause us to stagnate and become self-absorbed. Maybe that is why materialism is more dangerous to the believer than poverty. So it is best to see yourself as a grace giver first and foremost.

For those of us who have been graced greatly, much is required. That is why we need to understand that we have been graced to grace. As we have received, let us also be used to make an impact that is beyond our kingdom. Instead of seeing his grace to us as a sign of our deserving or being rewarded, let us see it as God gracing us to grace others. Remember always—we cannot out-give God.

CHAPTER 4

We Have Been Graced to Grace Others

GOD IS NOT GOING to ask us to do something that he has not personally already modeled for us and taught to us. So when we talk about grace giving, it all begins and ends with the ultimate Grace Giver of all, our God who is God alone. His Word outlines and models our responsibility regarding the grace that has been so freely bestowed on us.

Before I explain Genesis 1, let me emphasize that I take Genesis literally and believe it is God's account of how life began. Therefore, I will share what I believe God intended us to learn from this passage.

God in Creation

Right in the very beginning God established the principle of giving for us. On Day One, God created light. What does light do? It gives. It dispels darkness. It guides. It leads. It opens. The first created order was light that gives and receives nothing. "And God said that it was good." On Day Two, God placed the firmament in its place. On Day Three, God made the earth. Notice specifically what he said about the earth in Gen 1:11–12: "And God said, let the earth bring forth vegetation, the herb yielding seed, and the fruit yielding fruit after its kind, whose seed is in itself upon the earth, and it was so. And the earth brought forth vegetation, and herb yielding seed after its kind, and the tree yielding fruit, whose seed was in itself, after its kind, and God saw that it was good." Once again very early in the creation process, God made things that have one main function: to give. The primary function of the earth and trees was to supply their fruits to the rest of creation. As God met the needs of the earth by making it capable of giving (water, nutrients), God then made the earth and trees capable of being givers. What happens when a tree no longer gives off? It dies.

On the fourth day, God continued with his giving theme. He made the two great lights to rule the day and the night. Again, these are light sources. The sun rules the day and the moon, which reflects the sunlight, gives off light to rule the night. They receive and return what they have received. They were created to share what they have been graced with.

On Day Five, God created some of the animal kingdom—fish and birds. At the first, their simple mission was to be fruitful and multiply and fill the waters and the air. Yet after man fell into sin and the world-wide flood occurred, the animal kingdom took on a new role. Clearly God already knew all of this. This new role would be to give to mankind. Since then, every time you sit down and eat a piece of meat, you are the recipient of the grace of God. (And of course, every time you consume a vegetable or fruit, you are receiving God's grace.) No wonder we have been taught to say grace before meals!

On Day Six, God finished the animal kingdom with the land animals. Again God saw that it was good. (While later in Jewish history, God restricted what animals they were able to eat, the Lord later rescinded that law in Acts 10.) The animal kingdom was designed by God to be able to give to mankind what was needful.

Adam and Eve as Grace Givers

But God did something else on the sixth day. He created mankind. He goes into more exact detail of man's creation in Genesis 2. There are several significant truths about mankind that must not be overlooked. First, notice that mankind came into existence by earth giving of itself. God could have just spoken man into existence, but instead he took of the earth (the grace giver), and made man. Genesis 2:7 says, "And the Lord God formed man of the dust of the ground, and breathed into his nostrils the breath of life, and man became a living soul." Of course, the story does not end there.

Genesis 2 continues with Adam enjoying the garden and tending to it. Adam had to learn to give to the earth as well as expect from the earth. What tending actually required is not clear, but he had to learn to do it:

"And the Lord God took the man and put him into the Garden of Eden to till it and keep it. And the Lord God commanded the man, saying, 'Of every tree of the garden you may freely eat'" (Gen 2:15–16, NKJV). The trees were there to give to Adam. He did not deserve any of this. It was all about God the Grace Giver, giving to man, the recipient of this grace.

God then brought the animals to Adam, who was to name them. Adam had quite a vocabulary to name all the animals. (Naming the owl must have been a hoot!) Genesis 2:20 explains, "Adam gave names to all cattle, and to the fowl of the air, and to every beast of the field; but for Adam there was not found a help fit for him." Something was missing for Adam. So what did God do? He took the dust of the earth and makes a woman for Adam, right? Not at all. He performed the first surgical procedure with anesthetic and put Man to sleep and took from him to make Woman. There are so many significant components to that truth! Man learned right away that what he was given, he would be expected to share. God took from man to instill this thought clearly in his mind. It also taught the woman that she was a recipient of a gift from the man. She freely received, so she must freely give. From this event, the woman was brought into the world and she in turn gives life from her body to all the world, becoming the mother of all living. (Gen 3:20)

God, the ultimate Grace Giver, created all this to demonstrate his presence and spread his grace. Now here we are, thousands of years later, and all that he set in place still gives and shares just as God intended. The earth continues to yield its fruit. The animal kingdom regularly supplies food, clothing, and companionship for the hungry and needy. Mankind, which has been placed in charge of this earth and its food supply, must be the grace extender from God to others who do not have. Unfortunately, far too many are building bigger barns—hoarding the resources—and have not learned the lessons clearly stated in God's creative order.

Noah as a Grace Giver

I don't want us to ignore Noah as a grace giver. As a matter of fact, Noah became the first Biblical character to have grace associated with his name. Genesis 6:8 says, "But Noah found grace in the eyes of the Lord." Noah walked with God, and God poured out grace upon him that was unlike what anyone had received up to this point. What did Noah do with this grace?

He built an ark to give shelter, protection, and life to all its inhabitants. God taught Noah to give, and we today exist because Noah accepted the call to give of his time, talent, and treasures to be sure that man and animals would continue to exist. Noah found grace from the Grace Giver and extended that grace to the entire world. It is important to remember that Noah was a preacher of righteousness (2 Pet 2:5), suggesting that others had the choice to join in the grace gift of the ark, but his preaching fell on deaf ears. Nevertheless, Noah served well as the first man associated with the word *grace* in the Old Testament. Every board, every nail, every smear of pitch was applied out of obedience to his Grace Giver. He accepted the thought that as he was graced, he was to grace the world.

Abraham as a Grace Giver

In Gen 12 God calls a man by the name of Abram to leave his family, his people, and his homeland to become the father of the Hebrew nation. God was now moving from his general grace plan for the entire world, to a more specific grace action through one nation: the Jewish nation. Because of its importance, it would be fitting to include several verses here for us to see God's plan with Abram.

> Genesis 12:1–3—Now the Lord had said unto Abram; get out of thy country, and from thy kindred, and from thy father's house, unto a land that I will show you; And I will make of you a great nation, and I will bless you, and make your name great, and you shall be a blessing. And I will bless them that bless you and curse them that curse you; and in you shall all nations of the earth be blessed.

Did you notice the truths in this passage? We usually recognize the main thoughts: that God called Abram to be the father of the people of God and that he was going to make them a great nation, bless them, and protect them.

No people on the earth would be blessed as Israel was going to be blessed. Realize that Israel was:

- The only nation specifically given a land.
- The only nation specifically given laws on how to govern themselves.
- The only nation given prophets and judges and kings of his calling.
- The only nation to be given signs of their possession unique to them (Sabbath and circumcision).

- The only nation given a temple for God to inhabit.
- The only nation personally protected by God.
- The only nation promised a future.
- The only nation given the direct Word of God.
- The only nation to which he personally appeared.
- The only nation on which he put his name.

This list is only a beginning; there is more to the blessing of Gen 12. This promise was repeated with Isaac, Jacob, David, and the entire Old Testament. This was not a one and done deal. God gave Abram a promise that would be repeated throughout his dealings with his people, and we can be sure that what God promises, he keeps. He is a covenant-keeping God. There is a future for Israel, and God is not finished with them yet.

But I want us to notice the often-overlooked truths that are stated twice in Gen 12:1–3. The verses explain that God will make Israel to be a blessing, and in verse 3 he adds that in Israel "shall all nations of the earth be blessed." "All nations" would mean every nation that has ever existed, as well as every nation that presently exists and every nation that will exist. Once again we see how God grace gives to a people (Israel) with the expectation that that grace will be extended to others. But how have they been a grace blessing to the world?

Now that does not mean that they have not had their years of pain as well. But all of those sufferings can be attributed to a nation that has turned its back on its God. None of the sufferings would have occurred had they not rebelled (as often detailed in the Old Testament), or have asked that the blood of Jesus be on them and their children (Matt 27:25). The suffering to God's people has also broken his heart, but he chastens those he loves (Heb 12:6). Every follower of Jesus has had to experience some form of that chastening. God in his wisdom does as he sees fit.

Israel as a Grace Giver

It is not difficult to observe Israel as a grace recipient since there are so many incredible benefits historically of being God's chosen people. Yet we also need to recognize that the world has been blessed because of this nation. It is sad that so few ever recognize this vital truth.

There are, of course, the material blessings that have come to us from Israel. Just examine how many patents have originated from the Jewish community. Look at how many governments exist today on a constitution or ruling methodology that has Jewish roots. Consider the ethical parameters, dietary guidelines, medical remedies, and financial ideologies that have come from the Jewish community. Israel has given an immeasurable number of grace gives to the world, though they are often overlooked or ignored. The world owes much to God's chosen people for being a blessing just as God said that they would be.

But far beyond the basic life blessings are the spiritual grace gifts that supersede everything else. To help us remember these grace gifts better, let us begin each of them with the same letter and remember them as truly the ultimate fulfillment of Gen 12.

Monotheism

Israel's tenacity for the belief in one God has been a tremendous source of blessing in a world with more gods than can be numbered. Throughout Israel's history, particularly in the Old Testament, there was some struggle with the pulls of the world and their many gods. But by the time Jesus arrived on the earth, this belief was so strong in their thinking that on several occasions they picked up stones to kill Jesus because he alluded or stated Deity. By the way, he was, is and always will be God. Yet it is Israel's firm belief in monotheism (one true God) that lays the actual foundation for the Trinity. There is only one True God but he exists in three Persons; Father, Son, and Holy Spirit. Although most Jews do not accept the Trinity, they do understand that there is one and only one God (Deut 6:4).

Message

By message we mean the Word of God, the Bible. It is important to recognize that the authorship of Scripture was Jewish (with the possible exception of Luke). From Moses, the first writer of the Old Testament (some have suggested Job may have been first), to John, who wrote the Revelation of Jesus Christ, the authors were Jews. The Jewish writers were either eyewitnesses of the events, or received the records through oral tradition or Jewish historians. Regardless of how they received the information, all of the data was put together for us by Jewish authorship. They are also the people who copied it, protected it, and preserved it. If not for the Jewish community, the world would not have had the written communication from God. Through Israel, all nations have been blessed.

Messiah

Although the first two are amazing blessings of grace from Israel, the consummate fulfillment of Gen 12 is the Grace Gift of Messiah to the world. Messiah, although Jewish and although he came unto his own (John 1:12), is the Savior of the world. John 3:16 reminds us that "God so loved the world that he gave His only Son." Revelation 7:9 clearly pictures the blessing Messiah is to the world: "After this I beheld and lo, a great multitude, which no man could number, of all nations, tongues, stood before the Lamb, clothed with white robes, and palms in their hands." It truly appears that there will be a multitude of people in Heaven, all of whom will be there because of the Lamb, and that number will include some from every nation that has ever existed. (What exactly qualifies as a nation I am not sure, but as promised in Gen 12, Israel would be a blessing to all nations, and Rev 7 puts that in perspective reminding us of that crowd in Heaven.) What God promises he fulfills, even to the minutest detail.

Jesus as a Grace Giver

We have already looked at Jesus as the Ultimate Grace Giver as he poured out his life. His death on Calvary as a ransom paid to the Father on our behalf is a grace gift for which we will forever adore and worship him. But there is more to the Savior than his propitiation. His life on this earth was also an important picture of grace in action.

He modeled for us that which we are to emulate. We know how we are to behave in so many circumstances because we have seen our Savior live it out for us. Just think of all we have learned by watching him in action:

1. We learned to battle temptation.
2. We learned to submit to authority.
3. We learned to walk in holiness.
4. We learned to deal with opposition.
5. We learned to love others.

We Have Been Graced to Grace Others

6. We learned to practice humility.
7. We learned to obey the Father.
8. We learned to train others.
9. We learned to memorize Scripture.
10. We learned to finish well.

There are so many other truths that could be added here, but these at least give us a hint to the magnitude of the life of Christ. If he had only graced us with his death, that alone certainly would be cause for us to love and serve him. But he went further by giving his life as an example that we should learn to walk as he walked and talk as he talked. We know what it is to be a follower of Jesus Christ because we have seen him live it for us. His life covered for us what grace living is all about. Because we have seen him, we can be what God wants us to be.

His whole life was one of grace giving. He gave to those who thirsted. He gave to those who hungered. He gave to those who did not have answers. He gave to those who were demon possessed. He gave his life to the disciples. When he completed his life's journey, he had nothing of this world to claim as his own. He came into the world with nothing and he left this world with nothing (materially).

If we are to be a true follower of Jesus, should we not emulate him as far as we are able? One thing we can certainly do is give that which we are able to give. Jesus provides a very solid example in John 13. He is about to go to the cross and he is getting ready for the Passover meal on the evening of his arrest. He is gathered with his 12 disciples, and he grabs a towel and basin and washes their feet. What an amazing picture of our Savior giving grace to a people so totally underserving! In this audience of 12 are Judas who will betray him, Peter who will deny him, Thomas who will doubt him, and the rest who will run and hide because of him. Yet he rises from dinner and washes their feet. As he concludes this stirring example of service, he teaches them with these words:

> John 13:13–17, NKJV—You call Me Teacher and Lord, and you say well, for *so* I am. If I then, *your* Lord and Teacher, have washed your feet, you also ought to wash one another's feet. For I have given you an example, that you should do as I have done to you. Most assuredly, I say to you, a servant is not greater than his master; nor is he who is sent greater than he who sent him. If you know these things, blessed are you if you do them.

Notice clearly what our Lord has taught them. You ought also to wash one another's feet. There are many ways to wash feet, and what we need to do is simply see the grace that has been given to us as our means of washing the feet of those who have not the same privileges of grace. That could include a physical or spiritual need. Grace has no such limitations. What Jesus is saying is that all of us have the opportunity to get up from our graced positions and share the grace that has been entrusted to us. Our feet are clean because of grace. We have the towel because of grace. We have the basin because of grace. We have the water because of grace. We have the means because of grace. Without question some of the most joyful believers I know are those who share grace with others as their lifestyle.

Now this will require dying to self. The only thing that stopped the 12 from washing feet on that night was the fact that they were too busy trying to determine who was going to take over after Jesus left (Mark 10:35–45). Nothing is really different today—people get so consumed with their grace gifts that they forget the call of the Grace Giver.

The Church as the Grace Giver

The church, made up of blood-bought, graced people, is the recipient of grace that is not even measurable. And if you are walking the grace journey, you understand just how invaluable that daily grace really is. Where would we be without the grace of God? The problem isn't that we don't recognize that we have been given great grace—it's that we don't let that grace flow out of us. We who have been the most graced often find ourselves the least of the grace givers. We need to re-examine what it means to be those who have been graced.

The church is the bride of Christ. We are to submit to our Head and Groom who is Jesus Christ. Over time we come to resemble our Groom. Have you ever noticed how that couples over time begin to look like one another? (I feel sorry for my wife.) But in the marriage of the church and Christ, there is no question that we are to take on the appearance of our Savior. How does that happen as we journey in grace?

We Are Connected to One Another

A number of years ago I did a study on the phrase "one another" that is found in the New Testament. In my studies I had seen it often, and wondered how that it all measured out in the body of Christ. It was a study that has continued to bring my attention to this important connection that we have to one another. You can read more about that study in Appendix 2.

The church is called the body of Christ. When we think of a body, we think of arms, ears, eyes, and all other components that make up a body. As members of the body of Christ, we are also integrally connected and dependent on one another. No one member is more important than another, and all have their specific roles. But when one member pulls away from the body and becomes independent, it basically dies. Each member has been designed to serve the others. The hand serves the hair as it combs it. The feet serve the body as they take it places. The ears serve the body as they warn of incoming danger. The members of the body have been designed to not serve self, but to grace serve others in the body. First Corinthians 12:25 makes that clear when Paul writes; "that there should be no schism in the body, but that the members should have the same care one for another."

But the whole purpose of our position in the body is to use our grace gifts (the eye to see and the ear to hear, etc.) for those with whom we are connected. The only reason the eye can see for the body is that it was grace given that ability by God. The eye has no ability in and of itself, and it has no usefulness disconnected from the body. When each member remains connected to the body and functions in the way it is supposed to, the body is healthy. When a member of the body doesn't give, the body doesn't function properly. Notice some specific Scriptures that explain how we have been graced to grace.

- Romans 12:1–2 shows that by the mercies of God we present ourselves to God for his use.
- Romans 12:3 continues the thought that it is by the grace given to us that we have our position and therefore should not think more highly of ourselves since it is all because of his grace.
- Romans 12:4 explains that we are many members with different callings.
- Romans 12:5 then says that we are all members with one another.
- Romans 12:6 says " . . . having gifts differing according to the grace given to us." (How much clearer does Paul need to be?)
- 1 Corinthians 12:7 emphasizes that the gift of the Spirit is given to profit all (not self)

- 1 Corinthians 12:11 shows us grace gifted by his calling and his calling alone.
- 1 Corinthians 12:18 reminds us that we are set in the body as it pleases him.
- 1 Corinthians 12:25 encourages us to have the same care one for another.
- 1 Corinthians 12:26 explains that when one is suffering, everyone suffers; and when one rejoices, we all rejoice.

This is called the church. This is called the body of Christ. This is called the graced children of God giving out of their graced position to other members who are in need of the grace.

We Are to Love One Another

Although I mentioned it previously, I thought it would be best to expand on the idea of loving one another that was listed earlier. No "one another" phrase is used more often in the New Testament—the numbers aren't even close! "Love one another" occurs 15 times in the New Testament (John 13:34–35, 15:12, 17; Rom 13:8; 1 Thess 3:12, 4:9; 1 Pet 1:22; 1 John 3:11, 23; 4:7, 11, 12; and 2 John 5). I suspect that all the other "one another" phrases actually flow out of this one. But why is this one so repeated? Why does God have to tell us to love one another so many times?

The answer is simple: because we don't do it very well. Yet understanding our graced condition and the fact that we know love only because he first loved us ought to cause us to be the most gracious people on the face of the earth. The depth of our love, the depth of our forgiveness, the depth of his grace to us should spring out to these actions and attitudes to one another.

Just think about when you first fell in love with your mate. I remember those days well. I was still in seminary and living over an hour from my lovely fiancée. I was taking a full seminary load, teaching in the college, coaching the men's basketball team, and yet I had time to make my girl my priority. Why? Because I was in love. I was never too tired. I was never too busy. I was never so distracted that I was prevented from serving my lady. It is out of this kind of love that we need to minister to one another.

When Jesus was asked which commandment was the greatest, he responded with these words: "You shall love the Lord, your God, with all your heart, and with all your soul, and with all your mind. This is the first and great commandment. And the second is like it, you shall love your neighbor as yourself. On these two commandments hang all the Law and Prophets" (Matt 22:34). To this thought Paul adds: "But by love serve on another. For all the Law is fulfilled in one word, even in this; you shall love your neighbor as yourself" (Gal 5:13b–14). Love fulfills the Law, and as we recognize we have been graced, then out of our abundance of grace we should minister grace to others. This action pictures the church in its finest hour.

God Reminds Us to be Grace Givers

All throughout the Scriptures we have examples and principles given to us to teach us the importance and necessity of being a grace giver. Yet even with all of these examples, we often fall short of this calling. So our Lord offers another motivation to us by explaining that one day we will give account for the grace that has been given to us. We do not want to emphasize this beyond its intent, but the fact of the judgment seat of Christ is not something that we should take lightly.

As believers we have been greatly graced. Remember that it does not matter where you live or what your circumstances are, you have been graced abundantly. We still had to do something. Even if it was only our salvation (which is no minor display of grace), we are still greatly graced. Even if our time on this earth is full of pain, sorrow, and injury, we still have been greatly graced. And we must use the grace given to us.

First, just notice how many stories and parables Jesus taught that remind us that there is to be accountability for what we have been given. One such classic story is found in Matt 25 and called the Parable of the Talents. Here our Lord is the Grace Giver (as he always is), and we are the recipients (as we always are). He gives grace gifts, then leaves for a while, and afterward returns. It is very clear why he returns. After a long time the Lord of those servants comes and reckons with them (Matt 25:19). He has given gifts, and there is a day of accountability to see what we have done with those gifts. Jesus told similar stories throughout his ministry.

The epistles expand on this thought by explaining to us that one day every believer is going to stand before the Lord at what is called the Judgment Seat of Christ. Now we will not be standing there to give account of sin. Sin has been paid once for all by the blood of the Lord Jesus, and he remembers our sins no more. But we will give account of our stewardship of his gifts. These passages give some vital principles:

- Romans 14:10—"For we shall all stand before the Judgment Seat of Christ."
- Romans 14:12—"So then everyone of us shall give account of himself to God"
- 2 Corinthians 5:10—"For we must all appear before the Judgment Seat of Christ" that everyone may receive the things done in the body, according to that he has done, whether it be good or bad.

So let us take inventory of our own grace giving. Have you even been on the receiving end of a grace gift? I would imagine that you would have to say yes. Now, have you been a grace giver?

Who Should Receive Our Grace Gifts?

Believers. There is no question by our position in the body of Christ, that our first and major calling is be grace givers to that body. That is our strongest connection. Scripture even makes that statement for us: "As we have therefore opportunity let us do good unto all men, especially unto them who are of the household of faith" (Gal 6:10). Our serving, our caring, our loving, our grace giving begins at home. But that is not just a local assembly mindset. Our family truly exists all over the world; it needs our thoughts, prayers, and gifts. The New Testament church practiced this example for us.

When our brothers and sisters are persecuted, we need to carry that pain as well. When they are hungry and thirsty, we ought to be concerned. When they are martyred for their faith, it should not go unnoticed in lands where persecution may not exist. We as the church in the protected world have too long neglected our care for those hurting in other lands. It is time for the church in America to more consistently fulfill the grace needs of our global family. If we had an actual blood brother or sister who was hurting in a remote area we would do something about it. If my brother went to serve in Africa and was captured by Muslims, I can assure you I would not sit idly by. You would not, either. Well, we do have blood brothers and sisters that are all over the world and in need. These are our blood-bought brothers and sisters, bought by the blood of the Lamb. Why do we take their needs any less seriously? And just putting our heads in the sand will not suffice. I have heard believers say that they did not know a lot of what is going on all over the world. No excuse. We cannot fix all our family's problems, but we can certainly impact one at a time.

The story is told of one man who was walking along the beach after a strong storm. Hundreds of starfish had been washed alive up on the shore. This gentleman picked up one starfish at a time and returned it to the ocean. A couple of kids noticed the man's deliberate and tedious work as he moved ever so carefully among the many starfish on the beach. They called out to him; "Mister, what you are doing ain't going to matter. There are too many."

The man replied as he carried one of the starfish to the water, "It will matter to this one." Yes, there were more than he was going to save. But if he could only save one, that one would have been grace. The enemy causes us to see the needs as too great, and as a result, we are often paralyzed into doing nothing. Maybe we can only grace one. But that is one more than was graced yesterday.

Non-believers. Are we only to grace believers? Galatians 6:10 says that we are to do good to all men, and that would include the unsaved as well as the saved. God so loved the world (those without salvation), so why should we love any less? Sometimes grace giving might open up the doors for evangelism. As has been said, "They don't care how much you know, until they know how much you care."

Jesus gave food and water to the lost. He saw them as sheep without a Shepherd. He was moved with compassion when they were hurting. Jesus had much grace to give and he gave to many he came into contact with. He ate with the lost, visited the lost, touched the lost, ministered to the lost, and loved the lost. How can we do any less? And in our grace giving, evangelism must be a priority.

What Should We Do?

This all flows out of the truth that you believe first and foremost that you have been graced. We just had a special Good Friday service at our church where we developed a scenario similar to an underground church. We had the building dimly lit, chairs only for elderly, no heat/AC, and tried to give the feel of what our persecuted brothers and sisters may experience regularly when they worship. At the end we offered the opportunity to give

$30.00 per person/family to buy Bibles for believers all over the world who do not have them. Just a few days ago a family posted on Facebook how their kids raised money and were sending off their $30.00. My point in all this is to demonstrate that we all can do something because all of us have been graced to some level.

So, we all have been graced. In addition, we all have been called to grace others. Believers need to seriously pray about their "wealth" that they continue to accumulate and hoard all to themselves. Why do we not believe that grace has come to us simply for us to pass it along? And simply sharing it with your own nuclear family is not actually the same as grace sharing with the body of Christ. We should diligently evaluate how we use the grace given to us. The church has enough self-focus and self-centeredness. We don't need to supplement it anymore.

Two truths form our conviction. We have been graced, and we have been graced to grace others. Now what should that look like? It ought to flow out of us in two specific ways. First, we need to share what we have physically. Our material blessings need to be held on to lightly. All that we have belongs to him. We are bought with a price and are simply stewards of what he has graced us with. We own nothing, regardless of what the deed may say. When a member in the family is hurting materially, we need to seek his will to see if what we have been graced with ought to be shared with the hurting. When one member suffers, we need to feel that pain. If we can alleviate that pain we need to seek God's face carefully to determine if that is what he so desires. We are simply checking in with our Grace Giver to see what exactly he would have us to do with the grace things we have been entrusted. All of us have some grace gifts that fit into these categories. It may even require sacrifice on our part. Regardless, grace given to us is never meant to remain with us without his specific instructions to do so.

The second area where we need to consider grace giving is in the spiritual area. This area is an area that cannot be overlooked. God graces us with instruction. That instruction from his Word may come to us in many ways: teaching, preaching, reading, devotions, Bible studies, and more. It comes to us for us learn, grow, and mature, but that is not the final destination of these grace teachings. 2 Timothy 2:2 makes it clear that the things we have learned we are to pass on to faithful men. Nowhere are we to simply take it in and digest it for total consumption. Knowledge of this kind will only bring about pride.

We Have Been Graced to Grace Others

Jesus' last command to the disciples prior to Pentecost was to go into all the world and preach the Gospel. We have not completed that call. Maybe God wants us who have been graced greatly to go and minister to those who have little knowledge of the things that you hold dear. I am presently sitting in my office typing this manuscript and I have access to literally hundreds of volumes of works on all kinds of theological subjects. Many great men of the faith have taught me. Yet there are pastors laboring greatly for the Kingdom with little or no training and hardly any tools at all. Is this not to be my concern? I have had the privilege to share with many pastors overseas, and have made trips to Haiti, India, and Brazil. I do not say this to boast, because I have learned long ago if God uses me, it is all about amazing grace. I just point this out to let us be informed that there is much to be done and many needs to be addressed. I cannot get to all the pastors, but I can get to some.

We can share what we have learned so far on our journey with those who have so little, but we can also share the Gospel with those who are without Christ. Evangelism is every believer's responsibility; even if you don't think you have the gift of evangelism. 2 Corinthians 5:18 says that God has given to us (all believers) the ministry of reconciliation—bringing folks to Jesus. Every one of us has been graced to salvation, and if that grace stays only with us, the world has much to lose.

Can you list 10 people right now that you can bless/grace with the Gospel? They are all around us, in supermarkets, convenience stores, malls, the office, the school, the neighborhood, and all over. Someone graced you. Will you grace others?

CHAPTER 5

Grace Must be Applied

Grace in the New Testament

ONE DAY I HAD this grand desire to look up the word *grace* and all its cognates in the New Testament to examine just what Scripture says. I have to admit that although I have studied Scripture often, and this theme a few times, I was overwhelmed, awed, and humbled by the many statements Scripture contains about this subject. Being humbled is always a good thing since Scripture says he resists the proud but gives grace to the humble (Jas 4:6 and 1 Pet 5:5). And although I was very careful to look at every occurrence of grace in the New Testament, I doubt very seriously that I exhausted the information.

Below is what I discovered (for all the specific instances, see Appendix 1), but I would encourage you to take this same journey. You can research grace by using a *Strong's* or *Young's* concordance, or I would encourage you to purchase the *Word Study New Testament and Concordance*. This New Testament study book has every major word numbered to the concordance where you can examine every occurrence and notice every context based on its Greek usage. In the English, you may have a word translated differently than it really is in the Greek, and every translation has some level of interpretation. I would suggest you gather some helps that take you right to the Greek text.

If you go to the Greek text, you will find that the word *grace* occurs 156 times in the New Testament. Another, similar word which is typically translated as *gift* occurs 17 times. There is a verb that could be similar enough to be added here as well—our usual word for *forgive*. It is probably a different root word, but close enough that it connects in its 23 occurrences. The one verb that is clearly connected is only found twice. (Interestingly, the word *joy* is very close to the root as well. I wonder if that was intentional. It occurs 59 times.) I share all this to let you know that to study the word *grace* is not a simple endeavor, yet it is a very worthwhile one.

All we have and all we are is because of grace. Paul masterfully explained that he was who he was because of the grace of God (1 Cor. 15:10). We owe everything to grace.

- We are saved by grace
- We exist because of grace
- We walk by grace
- We stand in grace
- We are justified by grace
- We have what we have by grace
- We live because of grace

Additionally, when we die, there is dying grace – as the song says, "Grace will lead us home." No wonder we sing of "Amazing Grace." We owe it all to grace, but how few of us are truly living the grace life and how few of us are good stewards of this grace in that we are gracing others?

A Grace Acrostic

In Appendix 1, you can study about the many mentions of grace in the New Testament. Even reduced to 50 items, the very concept can be really overwhelming. Can anyone really understand grace? We, who have been the most graced of all people on the earth, will still be in awe of his grace when we get to Heaven. Grace might lead us home, but there is so much more grace awaiting us.

So let's try to make the concept easier to grasp, hopefully without diminishing its impact or importance. If you see the word as an acrostic, you'll be able to understand how grace is given to us as individuals and as a Church. Here is what it looks like before we add the explanatory verses.

G – *Given* to us

R – at *Redemption*

A – to *Act* upon it

C – that we may become like *Christ*

E – to benefit *Everyone*

G – Grace Given to us

It all begins with the understanding that all we have has been given to us, and grace certainly stands out as a major gift from the Lord. The children of God are a greatly blessed (given to) people.

Now it is also important to remember that our salvation is all about the work of God. Before the foundation of the world was put in place, the death of Christ was confirmed and orchestrated. He is the author of our salvation and he first loved us, sought us, and redeemed us.

Romans 5:1–2—"Therefore, having been justified by faith, we have peace with God through our Lord Jesus Christ, through whom also we have access by faith into this grace in which we stand." We stand in grace because of faith in him who has graced us. Peter adds, "that this is the true grace of God in which you stand" (1 Pet 5:12). Our position in Christ came about because of grace and now we can stand in him because of the grace given to us.

Romans 5:20—"Moreover the Law entered that the offense might abound. But where sin abounded, grace abounded much more." Because we were dead in trespasses and sin, we needed abounding grace. This grace, given to us at our salvation, is sufficient to declare us righteous in his sight. Paul even encourages the Corinthians that they need to abound in this grace (2 Cor 8:7).

1 Corinthians 15:10—"But by the grace of God I am what I am, and his grace toward me was not in vain, but I labored more abundantly than they all, yet not I, but the grace of God which was with me." Paul makes it abundantly clear that if anything good is happening from his life, it is all because of grace. It appeared at conversion and continued with him through the rest of his life. Hence Paul talks about laboring (using his God-appointed grace gift), to minister to others.

Ephesians 4:7—"But to each one of us grace was given according to the measure of Christ's gift." Wow, what a verse! He is clearly talking to believers since he is writing to the church at Ephesus, and his point is that each believer can stand in grace that is given to them at the time of their salvation. It appears in this context to refer mainly to the grace gifts that we share in the body of Christ, but I doubt we can limit it to the gift alone. We use the grace gifts all throughout our journey.

Titus 2:11—"For the grace of God that brings salvation has appeared unto all men." Everyone is aware of God's grace at some level, though not everyone is saved. Believers, however, should be increasingly cognizant of his grace as they journey through life.

1 Peter 1:10—"Of this salvation the prophets have inquired and searched carefully, who prophesied of the grace that would come to you." Peter reminds his readers that the prophets eagerly sought out (inquired and searched carefully) the grace that Christians have received. What an awesome gift!

1 Peter 3:7—"Husbands, likewise, dwell with them with understanding, giving honor to the wife, as to the weaker vessel, and as being heirs together of the grace of life, that your prayers may not be hindered." Paul emphasizes that fact that both the believing husband and wife are recipients of the grace of life. Now what exactly is the grace of life? I suspect that it refers to a reminder that a married couple needs to live out saving grace in front of each other and remember that both are heirs of this grace. Therefore, they are to treat each other with respect out of the grace they both share.

1 Peter 4:10—"As each one has received a gift, minister it to one another, as good stewards of the manifold grace of God." On this last one, can we just say, "Believers must use the gifts God gives them to minister to each other. That makes them good stewards of his grace."

We stand as people who have grace upon grace poured into us. Do you see yourself as one to whom much has been given, as we have emphasized repeatedly in the last several chapters? Well, whether you see it or not, you have been. No wonder the songwriter said, "Oh to grace how great a debtor/Daily I'm constrained to be." We are indebted for manifold grace that is beyond our ability to respond in a measure comparable to the gift.

Pause right now and begin to measure how much you have been given. Try to allow the Holy Spirit to point out to you how much you have been graced, blessed, given. Intentional evaluation can help us realize the totality of his grace-full intervention in our lives. I remember hearing about a man who wanted to sell his house, so he contacted a realtor. The realtor asked him to describe his house. After describing it for a half hour, the man suddenly stopped. He said he no longer wanted to sell his house, because he was describing the house he had always dreamed of owning! Recounting the details helped him understand what he really had. Maybe doing the same will help us understand the Grace *Given* to us.

R – Grace Given to us at Redemption

Our redemption was the act of the Savior buying us out of the world of the enemy. We were bought with a price. We were redeemed not with corruptible things like silver or gold, but with the precious blood of the Lamb without spot or blemish. He who knew no sin became sin for us so we could become the righteousness of God. That is the act of redemption.

There was a story I heard long ago about a family that had a terrible house fire. It occurred during the night and the fire spread fast and furiously. One brave firefighter went into the burning house and was able to save two young children. The parents died in the fire and there was absolutely nothing anyone could have done to save them once the fire was burning. The brave firefighter suffered some severe burns that sent him to the hospital.

Eventually, the town held a meeting to determine what to do with the children. One very wealthy and caring family came forward to claim the children. They mentioned their big house, their wealth, and their ability to care effectively for these children. As the town mayor began to ask for a vote, one more spoke up to claim the kids. It was the fire fighter. The mayor asked what he could possibly offer that would compare to this rich, caring family. The fire fighter simply rolled up his sleeves and showed his scars. That, my friend, is what our Savior did for us. He ran into the fire of sin and Satan and redeemed us for his own, and he has the scars to prove that. That was redemption. That was grace. (All verses in the next two sections are from the NKJV.)

Romans 3:24—"Being justified freely by his grace through the redemption that is in Christ Jesus." This verse summarizes so much in just a few words! We have been justified (declared righteous), and it was done freely (meaning it is offered freely), and it is all by his grace. The end result of this event was our redemption carried out by our Lord Jesus. His one act of redemption by grace was sufficient to declare sinners free from sin and free from condemnation. This is amazing grace. This same idea is repeated in several other passages:

- Romans 4:4—"Now to him who works, the wages are not counted as grace but debt."
- Romans 4:16—"Therefore it is of faith that it might be according to grace."
- Titus 3:7—" . . . that having been justified by His grace, we should become heirs according to the hope of eternal life."

Scripture also teaches that we have been called by grace. Galatians 1:15—"But when it pleased God, who separated me from my mother's womb and called me through His grace." Now some might say that this was unique to Paul, but I don't agree. In fact, Paul clarifies it later in his epistle to Timothy, his son in the faith. "[Jesus] who has saved us and called us with a holy calling, not according to our works, but according to His own purpose and grace, which was given to us in Christ Jesus before time began" (2 Tim 1:9). Our redemption began in eternity past but has become real time for us at the point of salvation. (It says we were redeemed before the world began because God sees time differently than we do. That is why Paul later adds in Ephesians that we are seated together in the heavenlies right now.) Our redemption by grace began before the world began and was imparted to us at the point of faith to be finally completed when our faith becomes sight.

Paul sums all this up for us in Eph 2:8–9, "For by grace you have been saved through faith, and that not of yourselves, it is the gift of God, not of works, lest anyone should boast." Our salvation from start to finish is all about his grace. We don't deserve it on any level at all, and He freely bestows it as a further demonstration that his grace is sufficient and amazing.

Since our salvation is all about grace, how can anyone think they can earn or merit it? There will never be enough works; we will never do enough good; we can never attain any level that would cause us to be accepted in him. He had to do it all. My friend, if you are relying upon anything other than grace to lead you home, you will fall short. Call out to him in grace. It is the only way.

A – Grace Given to us at Redemption to Act upon it

How many times does our Lord teach about accountability for that which has been entrusted to us? As mentioned earlier, he taught the parable of the talents where a master who had gone to a far country held his servants accountable for their actions while he was gone. Remember that in each of these stories, those who have anything in their possession only have it because it is given to them. They are required to act upon it.

Matthew West has just recently challenged the Christian community with that theme in his song, "Do Something." The video (currently on YouTube), discusses the story of a young lady who has taken on the burden of an orphanage in Africa. She understands that she has been entrusted with much, and therefore much is required of her. Each of you reading this book has been blessed and entrusted with grace. Are you acting upon it? It is clearly explained to us in Scripture that we were not graced to simply enjoy the grace, but to be a conduit for grace to flow through us to those who may need a grace encounter. We are God's grace agents every day and we need to see that as we journey this life, the people we meet are in need of the grace that has been poured into us. Again, notice the many passages that describe this action for us.

Acts 4:32,34—"And the multitude of those that believed were of one heart and of one soul; neither said any of them that any of the things which he possessed was his own, but they had all things common. Neither was there any among them that lacked; for as many as were possessors of lands or houses sold them, and brought the prices of the things that were sold." Now this is the church in action! Let me offer one word of caution: this is not some kind of spread-the-wealth socialist or communist idea. This is just materially graced people seeing those who are not as graced and recognizing that if they shared their more-than-enough grace, they would still have enough, and others would enjoy it as well! As I stated in earlier chapters, we cannot out-give God! So, as we grace others with the grace given to us, grace will continue to flow to us. He knows we can be entrusted with grace. What a plan God put in place! I wonder, do we still have the early church heart today?

Romans 12:6—"Having then gifts differing according to the grace that is given to us, whether prophecy, let us . . . " (several times in the next few verses the phrase "let us" follows the gift). We have been graced to "let us" act.

Paul repeats the idea in Eph 3:7: "of which I was made a minister according to the gift of the grace of God given unto me . . . " I have the privilege to minister (serve, grace others), because this grace was given to me with the understanding that it would grace others. Christians ought to be the most benevolent since we are simply passing along grace that has been given to us by a God who is gracious above measure. The writer of Hebrews expands this idea: "Wherefore receiving a kingdom which cannot

Grace Must be Applied

be moved, let us have grace, by which we may serve God acceptably with reverence and godly fear" (Heb 12:28). Remember that as we serve others, we are actually serving him. So, the grace flows right back to him.

2 Corinthians 1:12 really calls us to act with grace in all our efforts and endeavors. Paul says, "For our rejoicing is this, the testimony of our conscience, that in simplicity and godly sincerity, not with fleshly wisdom but by the grace of God, we have behaved ourselves in the world, and more abundantly toward you." Oh, what a call to God's people—to conduct ourselves properly, living out the grace that has been given to us! We have all the tools we need to demonstrate his grace to the world. When we don't, it is not the fault of grace that we have been blessed with (Eph 1:3). We simply aren't using it. Call upon this grace and behave with grace to a world that needs to see it in action.

It is sad to watch how believers treat each other and call it "contending for the faith." I believe we need to call it what it is—a lack of grace living. I wonder if our Lord was walking with us through the journey, would we treat our brothers and sisters the way we do. Let us go forth in grace and act out of grace.

2 Corinthians 8:1 confirms that even our "tithing" is in all reality an act of grace. Once again, we are simply giving that which has been given to us. First Corinthians 15:3 supports that same truth (liberality in KJV is actually the word *grace*). One of the sad commentaries on the church today is the lack of "tithers" in the church. The average church giver's tithe today is about 2.5 percent, rather low compared to the historic amount of 10 percent. I have known believers who gave no tithe at all year after year. While I realize that the tithe is an Old Testament concept, it is at least somewhat of a barometer of our heart's perspective. After all we have been graced with, why is it so difficult to give back to God? No wonder Jesus highlighted the widow who gave all she had out of her poverty. Since he owns it all, why is that such a struggle for us today? Maybe because we have moved from being grace dispersers to grace absorbers. It's funny; those who only absorb never seem to ever get enough, and those who give never seem to be able to give enough. It's your call!

Peter seems to bring this all together in 1 Peter 4:10 when he reminds us that we are stewards of the "manifold grace of God." It is in the context of the grace gifts that have been given to us. We were given grace by the way of gifts (salvation and service) at our redemption and our responsibility is to put this grace in action. Stewards are required to be faithful (1 Cor. 4:1–2), and I cannot imagine that our Lord is not going to hold us accountable for the manifold grace that he has bestowed upon us. Grace is never given without a great cost. It should not be buried in our back yard.

Now let me pause here for a moment to dwell on God and his expectations of our grace gifts. Yes, he will hold us accountable, but I can assure you that he is not up there worrying about whether we are going to correctly disperse his grace or not. He gives out grace simply as an act of love. How we respond is our act of love back to him. It is not that we have to grace others, but that we get the privilege to grace others. God has given to us and we get to give to others. What a privilege to be a conduit of his grace. Are you? Can you name those whom you have graced in the past week? Maybe you have become a grace absorber instead. Would your closest companions on the grace walk confirm that you are a grace giver?

C – Grace has been Given to us at Redemption so we can Act upon it, that we may become like Christ.

If in all our grace giving we make this all about us, we are so off base that we need to go back to the basics. There are many reasons why we are to be grace givers, but the ultimate goal in all is Christlikeness. In all that we do, we need to keep him as our focus and our goal. We don't grace because we have to, or because we get from gracing, but because as we grace others we are drawing to his likeness. Grace's ultimate goal is that we reflect the Grace Giver. We were made, saved, and graced to mirror him to others.

John 1 is the great chapter on the deity of Christ, particularly his incarnation. John 1:14 says that Jesus was full of grace. Now we have already demonstrated that grace existed in the Old Testament, but Jesus was going to be particularly recognized as the Grace One. I love how John puts in John 1:16, "And of His fullness have all we received, and grace for grace." Now what does that mean? I suspect that this verse is simply magnifying the two truths that believers enjoy. We experience personally the Grace Giver and he personally graces us with Grace. The overall emphasis is on him, the Grace Giver. We ought to emulate him as we walk this journey carrying his name (Christian). Are we full of grace and truth? Yes. Are we gracing others with that grace and truth? That is how we reflect our Grace Giver who has blessed us so much. Scripture in several places calls the grace that we have as his grace (Acts 15:11, Rom 3:24). Grace flows. It was never intended to stagnate. The intent is that it will impact others for his kingdom, and as

Grace Must be Applied

it flows through us, the ultimate goal is that we will become more like the Grace Giver. What a privilege that we have to not only grace others with what we have been given, but then to reflect he who gave it to us. Yet the more we hoard, the less we look like the One who graced us. What does our countenance say about us?

Let's permit Paul to explain this so well for us in Eph 1:3–14. It is a rather lengthy passage but I believe we need to see it in its entirety.

> Blessed *be* the God and Father of our Lord Jesus Christ, who has blessed us with every spiritual blessing in the heavenly *places* in Christ, just as he chose us in him before the foundation of the world, that we should be holy and without blame before him in love, having predestined us to adoption as sons by Jesus Christ to himself, according to the good pleasure of His will, to the praise of the glory of His grace, by which he made us accepted in the Beloved.
>
> In him we have redemption through His blood, the forgiveness of sins, according to the riches of His grace which he made to abound toward us in all wisdom and prudence, having made known to us the mystery of His will, according to His good pleasure which he purposed in himself, that in the dispensation of the fullness of the times he might gather together in one all things in Christ, both which are in heaven and which are on earth—in him. In him also we have obtained an inheritance, being predestined according to the purpose of him who works all things according to the counsel of His will, that we who first trusted in Christ should be to the praise of His glory.
>
> In him you also *trusted,* after you heard the word of truth, the gospel of your salvation; in whom also, having believed, you were sealed with the Holy Spirit of promise, who is the guarantee of our inheritance until the redemption of the purchased possession, to the praise of His glory.

Notice the highlights of this passage.

1. He has blessed us (graced us)
2. He chose us (our salvation and giftedness originated with him)
3. We were predestined unto himself
4. It is all through his grace
5. In him we have Redemption.
6. This particular passage does not emphasize how we are to actually Act out this grace, although his will is mentioned in several places

7. Again, ultimately watch how that all this is for him and his glory
   - In Christ
   - Chosen to be holy and without blame before him
   - Adoption of sons to himself
   - Accepted in the Beloved
   - Through his blood
   - His grace
   - His will
   - His good pleasure
   - He purpose
   - He might gather together
   - In whom we have an inheritance
   - Predestined according to his purpose
   - That we should be to the praise of his glory

How much clearer could he have made it? All that we are and all that we have is all about one ultimate direction and goal—that we give off a mirror image to a world that needs to see Jesus. If grace is not flowing through us, then it is staying in us, which means at least two things: 1) we are not gracing others, and 2) we are not becoming like our Grace-Giving Model. Only our God would devise a plan such as this—graced to grace.

Let's permit Peter's words to bring this section together: "But grow in grace and in the knowledge of our Lord and Savior, Jesus Christ. To him be glory both now and forever. Amen" (2 Pet. 3:18). The one who came full of grace and truth graced us so that we can live in this grace and grace others to be drawn to our Gracious King.

E – Grace has been Given to us at Redemption so we can Act upon it, but most importantly that we can become like Christ to benefit Everyone.

This has been explained in previous sections, but some truths can help cement the idea in our hearts. There is no question we are to do good to all men (Gal 6:10), especially the household of faith (believers). But this verse

Grace Must be Applied

includes all the people on the face of the earth. We are not simply to bless believers. Although that should be our first priority, it should not be our only one. The "body" image often leaves believers thinking that the only recipients of grace should be believers. Yes, the body of Christ should be a major expenditure of our grace, but ministering only to believers would cause us to miss much of what Jesus did as he fed, healed, and taught the multitudes during his ministry. Are we to assume he only fed and healed believers? As we live out grace, it ought to be a grace that is lived out among the lost as well as the saved. Should we only be Sunday gracers? The early church graced in such a way that their faith was contagious.

Luke tells us that we should witness to the lost as those that have been given grace and are grace givers. Acts 14:3 explains how he "gave testimony unto the word of His grace." That is evangelism at its best. We simply testify to grace—he, the Gracious One who would save the likes of us and who is more than willing to save the likes of you—is ready to pour out his grace into someone who is willing to empty himself so his grace can shine through undistracted. Then Luke adds in Acts 20:24, "But none of these things move me, neither count I my life dear unto myself, so that I might finish my course with joy, and the ministry which I have received of the Lord Jesus, to testify the gospel of the grace of God." Wow. As you reread this verse, absorb these truths:

1. If we get out of the way, we can be used of him.
2. The things of this earth interfere with us testifying of his grace.
3. We have received this ministry, whatever it is.
4. And we get to communicate that grace to others.

Only our Savior (our Grace Giver) could put together such a plan. Is there anything or anyone interfering in your life with your ministry calling to grace others? If so, now might be a good time to get alone with our Gracious Savior and get it right. Others depend on it.

There might not be a more beautiful passage picturing this than the one Paul gives us in 2 Cor 2:14–15: "Now thanks *be* to God who always leads us in triumph in Christ, and through us diffuses the fragrance of His knowledge in every place. For we are to God the fragrance of Christ among those who are being saved and among those who are perishing" (NKJV). The passage begins with grace. The King James version translates the word for grace in the Greek as "thank" in verse 14. Literally, we could say, "but to God, grace." Then he proceeds to explain how this grace fleshes itself out in the believer. He uses an image that would have been very real to the people of the day. Each Roman general had a fragrance that was particularly unique to him. For example, say that General Titus (fictional) used the smell of roses. When General Titus would conquer an area, he would bring the captives back to his place with chains and ropes and parade them through the town, after having poured his fragrance all over his captives. The smell was overpowering. Often the general would get home before an announcement of his coming was made. If it was a warm and somewhat windy day, the smell of roses would arrive before the king and his captives. You could be in your house and all of a sudden this aroma would hit you. You would know that it was the aroma of General Titus, who was returning with his captives. As he went through the town, the fragrance would grip the entire city.

With that in mind, reread the passage. Notice the important points:

1. It begins with God's grace in Christ.
2. Christ is our King.
3. He causes us to triumph (the difference in King Jesus and the kings of the world is that we want to be his captives).
4. He makes his savor (his particular fragrance) in every place.
5. For we are his savor unto the believer and the non-believer.

His savor (fragrance) is grace. It has been poured in us and on us. We are his grace scent to everyone on the face of the earth. All we come in contact with ought to be inhaling the fragrance of our King and should be drawn to him. We are captive to him and we are to actively give off a sweet aroma that blesses others and rises up to Heaven. Is this the way we are making a difference in the world?

Scripture lists a few examples of how this ought to be measured. Ephesians 4:29 talks about grace in our speech: "Let no corrupt communication proceed out of your mouth, but that which is good to the use of edifying, that it may minister grace to the hearers." Colossians 4:6 admonishes, "Let your speech be always with grace, seasoned with salt, that you may know how you ought to answer every man." Grace speech ought to be our regular way of communicating with others since we represent the King. We live on foreign soil. We are his ambassadors here on this earth. Paul adds in Philemon 7, "we have great joy and consolation (grace) in thy love, because the

Grace Must be Applied

hearts of the saints are refreshed by thee, brother." In other words, our presence should so grace others that they feel refreshed. What a difference we would make for the Kingdom if we saw our position in this world this way! Even praying for others ought to be an extension of grace (Heb 4:16). As we minister this way to others, we are truly what Peter describes as "good stewards of the manifold grace of God" (1 Pet 4:10).

God has *G*iven to us grace at the time of our *R*edemption that sets us apart from all others who live on this earth. As we *A*ct out this grace (let it live through us), then the world will see Christ in us, and the result will both *C*hristlikeness and world impact for *E*veryone. If we as his graced ones could truly follow this perfect plan he established, the world could still be turned upside down! You see, we have a great advantage over all the religions of the world. They have their methods, masses, and money. We have the wonderful grace of Jesus: grace that did reach us, and grace that is capable of eternal good.

CHAPTER 6

Scriptural Reminders to Keep Grace on Track

There Is More to Come

ONE OF THE MOST amazing thoughts about Heaven is how we will continue to learn, grow, and blossom into all that God desires us to be, knowing that we cannot possibly fully attain that goal. Heaven will be eternal, and we will still be receiving from our Lord. He is infinite, and although we will have glorified bodies and be without sin, we will not be God. There is only one God and we are not him. Heaven will be a continual growth on the journey to *know* our God, not to *become* God. In addition, Heaven will also be a journey whereby we will continue to enjoy grace, be graced, and grow in grace. Doesn't this also suggest that Heaven will be a place whereby we will continue to grace others? Will we still be gracing those around us with the grace that we have been given? Apparently so. So why not take this earthly time and practice gracing others, since we will be doing it forever? Let's look ahead at a few Scriptures.

Ephesians 2:7 states "that in the ages to come he might show the exceeding riches of his grace in his kindness towards us through Jesus Christ." Although we have been graced at redemption, we surely must understand that we have not exhausted his grace. There is more to come. There is no way on this side that we could ever have the fullness of any attribute or characteristic of God. He is omnipotent and limitless, and we are finite and limited. Can a one-gallon container hold more than a gallon? No, and neither can we clay pots (2 Cor 4:7) hold more than our volume will allow. Glorified bodies are not going to be God bodies, but bodies that are complete in Christ up to the measure allowed by a limited being.

First Peter 1:13 adds another thought, "Wherefore gird up the loins of your mind, be sober, and hope to the end for the grace that is to be brought unto you at the Revelation of Jesus Christ." Now what is this grace? It is more of the grace that we have been graced with from the time of our redemption. I suspect that in our earthly bodies we could only receive so much grace. When he appears (at the rapture) we are going to be given glorified bodies, which apparently can take on more grace. Somehow our tank will expand its grace capacity. If you think that his grace is amazing now, can you imagine what lies ahead for us? No wonder Paul said that "eye has not seen, nor ear heard, neither has entered the heart of man the things God has prepared for those who love Him" Maybe Jesus' statement he is going to prepare a place for us (John 14:1–6) might be referencing our new bodies that will be able to contain more of what he is anxious to pour into us. I cannot wait to enjoy what lies ahead for those who walk in faith.

It is wise for us to understand that we are not writing checks of grace out of an account that can be exhausted. In fact, upon our arrival in glory, there is much more grace awaiting us! I wonder whether the amount of grace distributed on earth could be connected to the amount of grace we'll receive in Heaven. In other words, the more we grace others, the more grace awaits us. This seems entirely logical since there are other, similar truths taught in the New Testament. For example, 2 Tim 4:6–8 suggests future reward based on present acts. However, I must add some important warnings that the New Testament gives about grace.

Warnings About Grace

You rarely see anything in print about warnings connected to grace. Grace is typically, if not consistently, portrayed as the beautiful gift that it is, but Scripture does not just paint the picture of beautiful grace without some cautions and warnings. Grace is certainly amazing and its benefits are incredible, yet we must listen to the Scriptures that discuss concerns about the abuse or misuse of grace. Any of God's gifts can be mishandled. We, God's children, are not the best stewards of the gifts that God gives us. We misuse spiritual gifts to our own advantage, we abuse power of church leadership (a gift from God), we abuse children, and we also abuse our bodies. How many believers are ineffective for the Kingdom because they have not taken good care of the temple given to them by the Lord? It was even hand-crafted by him personally (Ps 139). Yes, we have abused our grace gifts. So we need to heed the warnings that come with these gifts. Far too many just ignore them.

It Can be Abandoned

Paul was greatly concerned about the Galatians whom he had personally visited during his first and third missionary journeys. Much work had gone into those believers, and he was concerned that evidence revealed that they had actually strayed from the grace given to them at the beginning of the faith journey. Galatians 1:6 outlines his reaction: "I marvel that you are so soon removed from him that called you into the grace of Christ unto another gospel." The Galatian believers were going back under the Law and behaving as if grace had never come into their lives. Paul was in shock. Why would anyone walk away from grace? It makes you wonder if they ever fully understood it, but we need to keep in mind that Paul had been their teacher. If anyone knew anything about grace, surely it was the Apostle of Grace, since he wrote more about it than any other writer. He had taught them well, but the enemy is powerful and was luring them away from grace into legalism.

The Galatian warning is one we must heed carefully. Those of us who have been called by grace, saved by grace, justified by grace, and live by grace need to be on guard that we do not put ourselves under any other system. Paul continues his epistle by offering warnings to which we, as well as his Galatian readers, must adhere. I believe one of the reasons for writing this epistle was to warn believers from walking away from grace. Here is a sampling:

1. Be on guard against those who claim angelic communication—1:8.
2. Make sure you know the source of the message—1:12.
3. Beware of those who spy out your liberties to put you in bondage—2:4.
4. Be aware of those who have been extended grace—2:9.
5. Hypocrisy can carry you out of grace—2:11–14.
6. If works justify then grace has been nullified—2:16.
7. If righteousness comes by works then Christ died in vain—2:21.

Scriptural Reminders to Keep Grace on Track

8. Believers can be "bewitched"—3:1.
9. How you begin the journey is how you are to continue to walk—3:3.
10. The Law is not of faith—3:12.
11. Christ has redeemed us from the curse of the Law—3:13.
12. God keeps his promises—3:16.
13. We become his son by faith—3:26.
14. Our salvation is in Christ alone—4:4-5.
15. Don't let someone make a day more than it is—4:10.
16. Unwilling to hear the truth—4:16.
17. Don't be entangled with that which destroys our freedom in Christ—5:1.
18. Faith overrides false duties of legalism—5:6.
19. A little leaven (sin) wrecks havoc in the body—5:9.
20. Be careful to be around those who are trouble—5:12.
21. Your liberty is not an occasion for selfishness—5:13.
22. Disrespecting others limits our effectiveness—5:15.
23. Walk in the Spirit and you will not fulfill the lust of the flesh—5:16.
24. There are things we cannot do—5:19-21.
25. The Spirit will produce fruit in one who walks in grace—5:22-24.
26. We can be overtaken in a fault—6:1.
27. We need to think correctly about self—6:3.
28. We need to share what we learn, not hoard—6:6.
29. What we sow we reap—6:7.
30. We will reap what we sow—6:9.

While I have not exhausted this book's advice, you can see that it truly offers to the reader some clear warnings about removing oneself from the life of grace. The above list just details some of the effects of doing so. We see some of these in action today when a believer tries to live a life away from the protection of grace. Grace was never given to be temporary or optional. We have been graced and our position will always be one of grace. May we be as amazed as Paul was at those who so quickly fall away from grace.

Let me ask you—having begun the journey by grace (which is the only way the journey begins), have you been putting yourself back under the Law? Are you trying to live for God in any other way than the grace way? If so, you need to fall back on grace.

It Can be Received in Vain

The Corinthian church was certainly a puzzle to those who understood grace and the walk required of those who claimed to be followers of Christ. Their behavior often better exemplified lost people! Within this assembly might well have been those who profess and did not possess. That is true of many assemblies today. So Paul writes in 2 Cor 6:1, "We then, as workers together with him, beseech you also that you receive not the grace in vain." Obviously the warning clarifies the possibility of the action. If they are warned not to receive his grace in vain, then it is clear that it is possible to receive it in vain. What does that mean? The word "vain" can be translated as "empty." In other words, there was nothing following the profession of faith. There were no works demonstrating that true faith had occurred. And that can mean one of two things. One, the believer is struggling to move on with grace, or two, that the person is not even a believer.

How sad to go through this life missing grace altogether or missing the wonderful journey of walking in grace. If a person makes a profession of faith but does not follow it up with grace actions, then the grace is empty or in vain. Such a person makes no eternal impact and often causes much harm to the Kingdom as they profess faith but don't live it out. Be sure you have begun the true grace journey. If you are uncertain, why not begin today?

The story is told of a young man who had saved for years to go on a cruise. Finally the day arrived, and off he went on what he anticipated would be the trip of a lifetime. At the meal times, he would go to his room and eat peanut butter and bread that he had brought with him. The smells of the feasts all around would cause him much anguish, but he was still determined to enjoy the trip and stay on budget! Finally, on his last day as he was heading to his room for his last meal, a man asked him why he was not going to the feast. The young man said he had only paid for the cruise and not the food. The man laughed and reminded him that the price was all-inclusive. My friends, this is typical of some who have not learned to appropriate the grace of the Christian journey. How sad to walk the grace life under the Law and with little grace. That is not God's call for the believer.

Scriptural Reminders to Keep Grace on Track

It Can be Done Despite To

The wording of this heading might seem foreign to you, but I wanted to retain the King James wording since it strikes just the right note. Hebrews 10:29 says; "Of how much sorer punishment, suppose you, shall he be thought worthy, who has trodden underfoot the Son of God, the covenant, with which he was sanctified, an unholy thing, and has done despite unto the Spirit of grace?" The word means to insult. How would we be able to insult grace, and in particular, the Spirit of grace?

I suspect that we all may have done something like this. It would be to live out our lives for a time ignoring grace and living by anything but grace. We act ungraciously and trod underfoot all the Son of God has done for us. We do that which is unholy in a manner that causes grace to appear hidden or distant. The Spirit of grace (Holy Spirit) is to lead us from salvation on through the journey of being with Christ one day. What an insult to have begun in the Spirit and then to try to continue in the flesh (same warning as in Galatians)!

Try to imagine it this way. As a parent, you invest hours, days, and years into the formation of your child. But when that child becomes a teen, he or she walks away from all you have taught and modeled. True, because we are human we have made mistakes so the analogy breaks down, but the Spirit has led us perfectly and wisely, and we respond by walking away doing that which insults all that grace has shown us. Maybe that is why Scripture warns us about how we treat the Holy Spirit. We are warned not to grieve the Spirit (Eph 4:30), and not to quench the Spirit (1 Thess 5:19). May we learn that the Spirit intends for us to walk in grace, and he is committed to see us through this journey.

It Can be Blocked

Being a college basketball fan, there is little I enjoy more than a good rejection. Some kid comes down the lane anticipating a clear path to the rim only to have his shot sent into the fifth row. The crowd goes wild and the young man who thought he had an easy two, seems instead to be so startled he really is not sure what just happened. If you are the defender, that is a good thing. If you are the man on offense, it is an embarrassing thing. Similarly, Christians have the ability to send grace into the bleachers. How? James 4:6 explains, "But He gives more grace. Wherefore He says, God resists the proud but gives grace to the humble." Peter almost repeats the same thought word for word in 1 Pet 5:5, " . . . for God resists the proud but gives grace to the humble." Although there is debate over how exactly we can resist grace, one thing is for sure; no one in his or her right mind would want to do this. James makes it clear that there is more grace to be given to the believer but we have the ability to block it from coming. We do this by having a proud heart.

There are few things in Scripture that God hates, and one of them is pride (Prov 6:16–19). As a matter of fact, it is the first thing listed in his list of seven things that God hates. Just from these two passages alone we learn that God hates pride and pride keeps the flow of grace from reaching the believer. While there is no outlined program that suggests exactly how pride blocks the flow of grace, it is clear from these passages that it does. Here are the truths:

1. God hates pride
2. God has more grace to give to the believer along his grace walk
3. Pride causes God to resist the man who has this quality and therefore stops the flow of grace
4. While the humble believer receives more grace
5. Therefore a proud believer blocks grace into his life and subsequently into the lives of others

The consequences are staggering. As God looks for graced people to respond to grace calls, he must overlook the proud believer and move on to another. I suspect the pride is connected to the fact that the believer believes he does not need God or he thinks that the grace given to him was either deserved or earned. You can imagine God moving on from that kind of believer. For example:

- Satan fell because of pride—Isa 14, Ezek 28.
- Adam and Eve fell into sin because of pride and a desire to be like God.
- Israel fell because of pride.
- Satan tried to get Jesus to fall using pride as a temptation—Matt 4.

Pride is clearly one of the favorite tools in Satan's tool chest. No wonder God hates it and no wonder it stops the flow of grace in a believer's life. Just picture grace coming down the basketball court. Remember, you are on grace's team! But as grace attempts a pass to you, you deflect it and send it into the stands. Can you imagine how grace must be shaking its head? You walk off the court, losing the game, because you deflected grace when you should have been receiving it and passing it on. In the long run, God is still going to win the game, but how many believers are going to miss playing a key role in the contest because they resisted grace with their pride?

It Can be Failed (We Can Fail Grace)

Everyone fails periodically in their life journey. Maybe you failed a test. Maybe you failed a project. Maybe you failed an attempt at something. Today one of the rages on YouTube is "epic failure" videos. They show people doing somewhat stupid things and failing miserably. People attempt dumb things with trampolines, skateboards, and other sundry equipment, and the failure of these attempts is painful to watch.

The writer of Hebrews warns that the believer can fail of the grace of God. Hebrews 12:15 says, "Looking diligently lest any man fail of the grace of God, lest any root of bitterness springing up trouble you, and by it be defiled." That certainly does not look inviting for the believer. How can someone behave in such a way that they actually fail of the grace of God? If the verse can provide the necessary context, then the way grace can be failed for the believer is through bitterness and subsequent defilement that prevents grace from shining through. In the previous section, our concern was the fact that a believer can block the flow of grace by pride. Pride acts as a dam to the flow of good grace that is needed for the believer to be most effective in grace living. Here, the issue is different. The grace flow is not blocked *to* the believer, but the grace flow is blocked *from* the believer.

Have you ever met a bitter Christian? The story of Naomi in the book of Ruth just may be one of the clearest examples of a bitter follower of God in Scripture. Our story begins in Ruth 1 where a famine forces Naomi and her family to leave the Holy Land, and they flee to Moab. For reasons not shared in the text, her husband passes away. Her two sons then marry Moabite women, and again without explanation both young men die. Naomi (which means "pleasant"), has lost her husband and both her sons. Jewish law requires her husband's brother to marry and carry on the dead man's name (Deut 25:5–10). So Naomi returns to her homeland and Ruth, one of her daughters-in-law, travels with her.

Naomi doesn't seek to have the Mosaic Law applied to her; instead, she permits Ruth to receive the kinsman-redeemer benefit. One wonders why Naomi forfeited her right? Yes, she was older and probably past child-bearing years, but she was still the rightful person to receive the benefit. The answer lies in her response when her town began asking about her. Notice what is recorded in Ruth 1:20–21: "And she said unto them, call me not Naomi, call me Mara; for the Almighty has dealt very bitterly with me. I went out full, and the Lord has brought me home again empty. Why then call me Naomi, seeing the Lord has testified against me, and the Almighty has afflicted me?"

Several things stand out in her response. First, she asks that she not be called "pleasant" anymore, but "bitter." The word *mara* connects us to Ex 15 when Israel was traveling to the Promised Land and found some water they could not drink because it was bitter (Marah). Just as clean water was unable to flow for the people to enjoy, Naomi had stopped the flow of grace from herself to others. She was no longer able to be pleasant to people (grace people).

Second, notice whom Naomi blames for her situation. Four times in two verses Naomi lays her blame at God's door:

- "The Almighty has dealt very bitterly with me."
- "The Lord has brought me home empty."
- "The Lord has testified against me."
- "The Almighty has afflicted me."

Not only was Naomi stopping the flow of grace out to others, she was also personally feeling the effects of her sin. Bitterness is such a crippling sin in a believer's heart. That is why Hebrews warns against bitterness springing up in our hearts and defiling us. Grace must never be prevented from flowing to those in need. How sad when a child of God becomes so resentful toward him that they miss out on the bounty of his grace!

I am not suggesting that believers don't have difficult times. I can only imagine how hard this must have been for Naomi. She had left her family and friends and gone to a pagan nation. She saw her three family members die (and we don't even know how). It may have been under tragic circumstances. Now she returned embarrassed and lonely. Did she have cause for pain? Absolutely. Did she have cause for bitterness? Absolutely not. Did she have cause to blame God? No way.

Job's response to suffering was the exact opposite of Naomi's. He also had great loss and suffering and pain. He lost his oxen, donkeys, servants, sheep, camels, sons and daughters, and his health. Yet listen to Job in Job 1:21–22: "Naked came I out of my mother's womb, and naked shall I return there. The Lord gave and the Lord has taken away; blessed be the name of the Lord. In all those Job did not sin, nor charge God with wrong." (NKJV)

Job kept the grace flowing out of him. In the following chapters he is able to grace his friends in numerous places and in the end, God blesses him so that he was blessed (graced) more in the latter end than at the beginning. So Job died being old and full of days. He died a blessed man and a man who was capable of blessing others right up to the end. Sadly, Naomi was not able to do that because bitterness prevented her from being able to do so.

I would imagine you know of some examples right now of believers who have stopped the flow of grace due to bitterness. It is so sad to observe. But let me probe a little further—have *you* stopped the flow of grace? Maybe you don't even know you have become a bitter believer? Maybe you need to take a more serious look at the grace flow. If it has slowed or stopped, there is a good chance bitterness is the problem. You cannot afford another day of grace stoppage.

It Can be Turned

Jude 4 gives us a strong warning of how the grace of God can be turned from its original intent (blessing) to an improper application (such as denying God). The text warns how it can happen, and it seems to be connected with ungodly men who have evil motives and end up in the assembly of grace believers. It is the same word used of Enoch's translation. Here Enoch is, and then he is gone. Here grace is, then it is gone. The thought is that grace, instead of promoting godly living as it should, instead has led to ungodly living. It is similar to the warning Paul gives in Rom 6. We conclude: "If I am under grace, I am covered and can basically do whatever I want."

True, I am saved, secure, and graced. Nothing can separate me from his grace. But grace was never intended to be used as a license to sin. Grace's purpose was to take the sinner that we are and move us from sinner to saint. Grace is sufficient to cover all of our sin. However, ungodly men can turn this grace from its intended plan for the believer.

Now this is not grace's fault. Grace has done nothing wrong here. Grace is amazing and the blessing God intends for it to be, regardless of how sinful and disgusting we can be. Grace that has been turned into ungodly lascivious living is a picture of what sin can do to mar what God has magnified. We need to be cautious about our living. Are we living grace lives in awe of his blessing or in a life that is pushing the limit of God's grace?

Jude adds several examples of those who pushed the grace limits and suffered the consequences. His first, most poignant example is children of God who were destroyed for lack of belief in the wilderness wanderings. Here were people who were positionally the people of God, but practically not living it out. God's people cannot play fast and loose with his grace. Doing so brings consequences that were never intended for his children. Are you playing with the grace of God?

I trust that these reminders will cause you to keep a close watch over grace and guard its God-given intent. Grace should not be taken lightly (neither should any of our gifts from God). What cautions should be put in place in your life to ensure that grace will be all God intends for it to be for his glory in your life?

CHAPTER 7

Barriers to Grace Living

THE QUESTION I OFTEN ponder about grace is why more of us don't live the grace life and extend grace more often. We know this is God's plan for us and when we do so, life is so much better. We will look at some of those benefits later from grace but for now, just pause and think of all Scripture says about those who follow the Lord and live the grace life.

1. It is freeing—not under law but grace
2. It is joyful—how often joy is connected to grace
3. It is Christ-like—Jesus came full of grace, and when we live grace, we are certainly living like the One who modeled living like this for us
4. It is attractive—just see how the early church turned the world upside down by living out grace in front of a world that cannot understand such behavior.

We could add so much more (I will do so in chapter 9). But for now, just allow the Holy Spirit of Grace to move in your hearts and see the many benefits of grace living. The opposite means living without grace or without sharing grace and no one sees any such benefits from such behavior. Then the question follows: why don't we do better at grace living?

The Obstacles

Obstacle #1: We are self-consumed

Have you ever noticed that self is the most hyphenated word in the English language? Look it up some time. Here is a partial list to get you thinking in that direction.

Self-consumed	Self-absorbed
Self-centered	Self-contained
Self-absorption	Self-addressed
Self-assertion	Self-collected
Self-conceit	Self-confidence
Self-conscious	Self-defeating
Self-destruction	Self-driven
Self-delusional	Self-determination
Self-destruct	Self-devotion
Self-educated	Self-employed
Self-esteem	Self-fulfillment
Self-hate	Self-help
Self-improvement	Self-interest
Self-made	Self-propelled
Self-preservation	Self-realization
Self-regard	Self-respect
Self-satisfying	Self-starter
Self-support	Self-sustaining

In the *Webster's New World Dictionary* (which I highly recommend simply for the name) there are 137 individual listings for self and a word attached to it. Not all are bad terms. Certainly some are actually good words such as *selfless*, but for the most part, we are a society consumed with ourselves. Most of the 137 entries are somewhat incriminating. We are a society that loves ourselves. If you don't think so, let me suggest a few ideas for you to consider.

First, go into any prominent bookstore and ask for the self-help section. You will find a plethora of books covering just about any self-help topic that you could ever imagine. True, not all of these are useless. For example, you can find books about how to do most anything you would want to do, such as gardening, photography, or construction. These books are intended to help us do many things that we have a desire to do. That alone is not a bad thing.

But I believe it is a symptom. Ask the staff at the next bookstore you visit for the "dying to self" section. Their first reaction may be to call 9-1-1, since they might just believe that you are mentally unbalanced or turning to self-harm! But have you ever considered what the Scriptures teach on self? In my doctoral studies, I did a graduate thesis on the Biblical view of self-esteem. Needless to say, it was not a best seller. No book publisher called me up after reading the document asking to print it in hundreds of languages or put it in every bookstore. Of course, one reason may have been how poorly it was written grammatically and organizationally, but the major reason was undoubtedly the content.

Yet dying to self is clearly the message of Scripture.

Matthew 4:18–20—Jesus called his followers to leave self (whatever consumed your past life) and come and follow him.

Matthew 10:32–42—Whoever reads this section and beliees we need to esteem self has obviously a different understanding on the passage than meets the eye. Notice what Jesus clearly says in these verses:

1. Whoever loves family more than Me is not worthy of Me
2. Whoever does not take up his cross is not worthy of Me (if you saw a man in Jesus' day carrying his cross you knew what it meant – that was a dead man walking)
3. He who loses his life for my sake will find it (loses his life – dies to his life)

Matthew 16:24–26—Jesus again repeats some of the thoughts we discussed in chapter 10. But unless we again miss his main points let me point out the more obvious ones to us.

1. If anyone desires to come after Me, let him deny himself
2. Take up his cross (same meaning as above)

3. Lose your life – how much clearer can it get?
4. What profit if a man gains the whole world (esteeming self), and loses soul. Toby Mac has great song on this theme: I don't want to gain the whole world and lose my soul. How many have chosen to put self first and live for self and be consumed with self? Sad, but even more sad is when a true believer loses sight and becomes so enamored with self that he or she becomes blind to their self-centeredness. It is a true block to his grace.

Luke 14:25–35—What a passage. It seems to sum up all of what Matthew had been saying. Again, look at the main points:

1. Hate family (Matthew explains that it means to love God more)
2. Hate his very own life (where does that fit into today's pop view of self?)
3. Bear his cross (dead man)
4. Count the cost
5. Forsake all (including self)

The apostles and early followers truly got Jesus' message. Just look at what happened to them for choosing to be a follower of Jesus according to tradition:

1. Stephen: stoned to death
2. James the Great: beheaded
3. Philip: crucified
4. Matthew: slain by a halberd
5. Mark: burned to death
6. James the Less: stoned
7. Andrew: crucified
8. Peter: crucified upside down
9. Paul: beheaded
10. Jude: crucified
11. Matthias: beheaded
12. Bartholomew: crucified and beheaded

13. Thomas: thrust through with a spear
14. Luke: hanged
15. Simon: crucified
16. John: exiled

These died for their faith and commitment, and considered it a pure joy to be able to suffer for the cause of Christ (Acts 5:41).

There are many other passages cited that could be cited in the New Testament that basically express the same point. Here are just a few:

- Romans 12:3—There is a warning not to think too highly of self. Obviously a problem we must encounter and deal with.

- 1 Corinthians 6:20—We are not our own. How can we esteem what does not belong to us?

- 2 Corinthians 4:7—Not much value in earthen vessels (clay pots). Our value comes from what is inside – our Lord and Savior.

- Galatians 2:20—How much clearer does Paul need to say it?

- Philippians 2:3-4—Esteem others better than self.

- Colossians 3:3—For we are dead. Note that this is written to believers. We should not spend our time on that which is dead. Many of us have read stories or seen movies where the medical community came upon an accident of some sort and began dealing with the casualties. Now would it make sense to be working hours on a body that was already dead? Of course not—they work on those who are still alive. Yet many believers do just that.

This life is not ours. This world is not ours. This kingdom is not ours. Yet many believers live lives that would suggest just the opposite, and they instill these same sentiments into the lives of their children. I have watched the parenting process for years and have seen this attitude become the norm (If you're interested, you may want to read my book, *I Heart Parenting*). By the time the child hits middle school, the parent wonders why they are so self-centered. Well, let's think about it.

1. Every birthday is a major event with each year becoming more monumental. The gifts, the toys, the places where the events occur. I have attended parties where I encouraged the family to just put some of

those toys away and bring out for a rainy day. It is almost embarrassing. No one child can play with all those even if they tried.

2. Every sporting event crowns a winner it seems. Even after a losing season there are party and trophies and pizza as if they just won the championship. They may have been a sorry team, but there are trophies for all!

3. We have been fortunate to go to Disney World, and it was quite eye opening for us. We would not go when the children were too young to enjoy it. It simply is a status and prestige thing for some. We have seen parents dragging small children around and basically saying to them, "You are going to enjoy Disney because I paid so much for this. Who cares whether you're only 3 years old!" But the main point seems to be that we are committed to giving our kids everything we can to make life special for them. I am not against gracing our kids, but not if they become selfish in the end.

4. Every event of the child gets posted on social media. First tooth, first steps, first poop. The child has a portfolio by the age of 3. I wonder why they are so self-centered.

5. If you think I am overstating it, then just consider the currently-popular phone craze of "selfies," where someone takes a picture of him or herself with or without other people. Then that person posts the picture on social media, mainly to glorify themselves. If you don't think that is true about social media, just take a careful look next time. People are either bragging about their children, grandchildren, themselves or some personal glorification. Here we are at the beach. Who cares? Here we are at the Mexican Restaurant. So what? Here we are at my son's little league where he is the best player. Really? OK, so maybe I stretched it a little, but not much. We are a self-focused world.

Where is the teaching on dying to self? Where is the teaching on his Kingdom? Where is the teaching on self-sacrifice? Our kids cannot get it if it is not modeled and taught to them. I have periodically asked seniors in high school what they plan on doing after high school or college. I rarely ever hear a teen say, "Whatever God wants me to do. I'm thinking of _____, but I want to follow his leading." Instead they go to graduation and hear how wonderful they are and how they are going to take on the world and do great things (you can see why I am not asked to speak at graduations).

We need to be preparing servants for the King, not servants for self. God does not measure our greatness by how many servants we have, but how many we serve.

How are we getting this so upside down? We have a Savior (Lord, King, God, Leader, etc.), who has called us to die to self, but we are esteeming self. Where are we going astray with this fundamental teaching of our Savior?

One final thought that needs to be explained under this section on self is why this whole concept matters. So I am too self-inflated. What does that have to do with grace? Grace should be seen as a gentle flow from the Savior to a willing vessel. He is always more than willing to share grace. Are we more than willing to receive it and share it? The problem with selfishness is that it sends a message to the Grace-Bestower that we are fine and in need of nothing. It is similar to our Sunday-morning church conversations. How many well-meaning people walk by us and ask how we are doing? (I am not going to judge why they ask; many certainly have pure motives.) What I believe ought to be examined is our answer. You might believe, for example, that people don't really want an answer to this rhetorical question, and you may be right. But does that justify our answers, which are usually something like: "I am great . . . fine . . . ok . . . doing well . . . super . . . better than I deserve [from the more spiritually minded]"? We may just have received horrible news, or had a major fight at home, or a speeding ticket on way to church. But our response is typically the same.

That is how it appears to God when we tackle things by ourselves and basically keep him at a distance because we can do it ourselves. I remember a parent once telling me that her little independent child often used the phrase "I do it own self" when she asked if he wanted help. Oh, how we establish our independence and island mentality early on with God! As a result, we block the available grace we so desperately need as we attempt to walk this journey all by ourselves. We cannot do it ourselves, and we need to fall on his grace moment by moment. Our selfish society puts grace on hold for the journey.

Obstacle #2: Pride

Now many may connect being self-consumed with pride, and the ideas truly are connected. But I believe self-centeredness might just be the tip of the iceberg, while pride is the vast mountain of ice just underneath the surface. That is why I chose to keep them separate. Many might say that they are too self-focused because it is hard to die to self in this egocentric society. But society isn't the root cause of our self-centeredness. The reason is pride, and it is much more evil and seductive than selfishness. Selfishness exposes stubbornness. Prides exposes our arrogance.

We have looked at pride in earlier sections, so I won't labor the point here. I just want you to see how pride and selfishness connect. Perhaps you wonder which comes first – pride or selfishness. I believe pride is much more serious and takes longer to develop than selfishness. So, the enemy sows the seeds of selfishness early in the lives of children. As they grow into such a world, they then begin to have an entitlement mentality, again fostered by everyone around them.

The McDonald's slogan used to be: "You deserve a break today." They targeted young families and kids. They encouraged you to bring your family and give your child a meal with a toy. Great marketing. Then they put a playground inside so coming to their place was such a happy event. The parents got to relax and eat, and the children could play. What parents would deprive their children of such fun? Now I am all for fun, but when has this become something we all deserve? Our Declaration of Independence got it right when it said: "We hold these truths to be self-evident, that all men are created equal, that they are endowed by their Creator with certain unalienable rights, that among these are Life, Liberty and the pursuit of Happiness." Life and liberty are our rights, but happiness is not, only the pursuit of happiness. The Bible adds a similar thought when it says, "having food and clothing be content" (1 Tim 6:8). Does anyone really believe that this generation would be content with those few items? How about just life and liberty and the ability to pursue happiness, whether we get it or not?

Our entitlement society says that the government needs to provide for us whatever we believe we ought to have. Even today we are experiencing a people that believe the government ought to provide food, clothing, shelter, and health care to anyone who is struggling to get it. This kind of spirit is very dangerous. You can never give enough to those who believe they ought to have to satisfy their quest for more. It is called pride.

An opposite but equally as deadly manifestation of pride is where people feel they can do everything themselves, on their own strength. Such arrogance puts God on the back burner. That is why God hates pride and gives grace to the humble (Jas 4:6, 1 Pet 5:5). Pride is a showstopper for God, and that certainly makes sense. Would you give to someone who does not think that they need any help? "I can do it myself" is their slogan.

Unbelievers often chastise Christians in this area, because they suggest that Christianity is a crutch. Christians, they feel, are weak people who are unable to "do it themselves" and need a crutch—Jesus Christ—to cling to. They, in contrast, do not need such a weak-minded support and therefore can do this all on their own. It is the epitome of pride.

It is pride that prevents the lost from coming to faith in Christ. Many often even resort to the thought that they can get to Heaven on their own. Now is that not an amazing statement of arrogance and deceit? God, who is above all, is going to let sinful man in his presence just because he exerted an effort and did some good? Oh that man would fall on his face and humble himself before God so that God in his grace could redeem him and set him free. Pride just gets in the way.

Obstacle #3: We love law.

Now before someone yells at me for such heresy, let me explain. Mankind overall needs boundaries. We like lists. We like laws. We like the do's and don'ts. Now why is that? Because we like to measure how we are doing. If there are Ten Commandments, how good are we if we obey seven fairly well? In most colleges and universities 70 percent is a passing grade. Would not God pass us for such a grade?

Grace does not measure well, and that is intentional. If we have to go around measuring how we are doing with grace, then we have missed the whole picture of grace. Grace is not something that has a barometer. Just picture grace for a moment from God's view. As he ministers grace to us, does the amount of his grace diminish? Of course not. I love the old song that says just that: "His grace has no limit." It cannot be exhausted; neither can it be measured.

Now that makes it hard for us because we are list- and boundary-oriented. Since grace is neither, we often attempt to drift from grace into lists and standards. God never intended for us to go down that path. Yet it never hurts to let Scripture measure us under the inspiration of the Holy Spirit.

God wants us to learn to walk in grace, yet grace flows contrary to our very nature. No wonder Paul and others began their epistles with "grace to you." As hard as it is, we must learn to walk the grace life, overcoming all barriers that limit it. To further explain this, let's remember why the Law came in the first place. Adam and Eve were given one basic prohibition. This law should have been manageable, but they failed. As each day went by, they could have evaluated their walk by saying, "Another day and no eating from the tree. We are doing well." Yet with just this one thing, they could not measure up. Their sinless walk did not last forever and because of that, God had to administer grace.

The Law given to Israel through Moses was the same. Mankind found out that although they had the list they wanted, they could not measure up. The religious elite in Jesus' day tried to even give specific details to the Law so they could be seen as righteous and above reproach. Of course they were whited sepulchers, full of dead men's bones. They had so blinded themselves to their unrighteousness that they believed that they were better than everyone else. Grace cannot be evaluated that way. There is no list and no written report. Grace is grace, and our worst enemy in living it out lies within us.

So maybe it is better to say we like law because we can measure others by it, while not really measuring ourselves. And he who compares himself with others is not wise. The standard for grace, if we really want to apply one, is Jesus Christ. May we all take on the grace journey for his credit and honor and glory. Because when we truly live the grace life and extend grace to others, it has nothing to do with this earthen vessel, but what lies within—our Gracious God and Savior, the Lord Jesus.

How sad that there must be a chapter on grace barriers. That which God has so freely bestowed upon us and that which so much describes him in all his compassion to us is often greatly misunderstood and resisted. It would be beneficial if every believer would take some quality time in the presence of God and ask the Savior about this great gift of grace and just how he sees it being used for his glory.

We need to walk this grace journey with eternity in our eyes, realizing that we only have one lifetime to get it right. Yes, a lifetime seems like a long time, but as James so beautifully writes, "Live is a vapor." Oh to grace how great a debtor. May we live this journey with great care and honor to our Gracious God. Do you want to get it right?

CHAPTER 8

Benefits of Grace Living

What if I Don't Grace Others?

BEFORE I SHARE THE benefits of grace living, let me pause to discuss the consequences of not gracing others. I am not sure we take this seriously enough. There is much to suffer both personally and corporately when we withhold grace from those around us.

A failure to grace others may reveal a lack of personal relationship with the Lord. Why is it that we who have been graced so much struggle so hard at blessing others? We may even have to ask whether we have a personal relationship with God at all.

The Apostle John explains how it should work: "By this we know love, because he laid down his life for us. And we also ought to lay down *our* lives for the brethren. But whoever has this world's goods, and sees his brother in need, and shuts up his heart from him, how does the love of God abide in him?" (1 John 3:16–17, NKJV).

It's a fair question. James discusses the same thought in James 2. If we say we have faith and do not practice our faith (grace living), does that faith save us? If we see a brother or sister in need and do nothing, that is graceless living. That is faithless living. I believe it accurate to say that if you have no burden, concern, care for those who are hurting, struggling, or in difficult situations, then you have a questionable faith. You cannot dismiss this lightly. A lack of care and action reveals a heart that is distant from the Savior. What makes you think you have faith at all?

But for the sake of fairness, let's say you do have faith, but just are not practicing grace living. Is that a possibility? I will let you work that out on your own in front of the Holy Scriptures with the Holy Spirit as your guide. He is the One who is to either confirm your salvation or caution you about your lack thereof (Rom 8:16). My word of warning is that you are on dangerous soil to believe you can have all the grace afforded to a believer and share none of that with anyone. But there will be those who will be ashamed at his appearing (1 John 2:28), and there are those who will receive no reward at the judgment seat of Christ. How sad. Those who have been graced so much and to whom much is given much is required. May we determine that grace will flow through us for his glory.

Consequence #1

The first consequence of failing to grace others is a personal failure and limitation. Now we often don't like to think of the personal side of an action because it sounds so self-serving, but in this case it is a challenging way to think of grace. God never intends for us not to have personal benefit on this earth. He came to give us life and to give it to us more abundantly (John 10:10). But far too many believers have no joy or abundant living. Grace flowing from us to others makes us some of the most abundant living followers.

Have you not noticed that those who give the most have the most joy? Is that a coincidence? Of course it is not. Grace living and grace giving is the God ordained path for the believer. He who finds this path of grace and lives it will also find the blessings that go with it. He who resists and does not will have as its consequence the lack of the blessings that come from grace living. Sad that many will never know what they are missing.

Consequence #2

By failing to administer grace and live the grace life, we limit (hinder) the glory of God on this earth. We are told to do all to the glory of God (1 Cor 10:31). We also know that our Lord laid aside his glory to be here in the flesh (John 17:5). God's glory is most apparent when his church lives the grace life. Therefore, Paul exhorts us to give God glory and to do all for his glory. Yet when we fail to live out grace, we hinder his glory.

Besides being a directive of the Lord, it's important because as the world sees him high and lifted up (glorious), the lost are drawn to him.

That is why the early church was so effective. They lived out grace and gave him the glory, and many were added to the church. I don't believe we can separate those who came to faith in Acts 2 from the grace living of the church. Caring and serving and loving one another in such a way made the cause of Christ contagious. You can be sure that there were many who came to faith simply because they saw something in action that appealed to them.

Too often, however, the church strays from the mandate of appealing to the lost. Instead we become consumed with arguing, fighting, and legalism. I have seen that over and over again. It has become alarming. Let me share a few examples. I remember once incident a while ago where I mentioned a certain writer in a message. After the message, some well-intentioned member chastised me because this author was a "neo-evangelical." Most recently, after I read a tremendously challenging book and encouraged our church to read it as well, I had some warn me that he was Amillennial and they were concerned about his theology. (By the way, there is nothing in that book that has anything to do with Millennialism.) I am just using these as a marker of concern. We are so busy fighting in the body of Christ that we have little time to live out the grace life.

I wonder what would happen to America if we began to experience the persecution that other nations endure? Would we go underground and have a litmus test for who we would allow in our particular group? "Sorry, you are Calvinist and we don't worship with your kind." "Sorry, you are Charismatic and we can't have that in our group." "Sorry, you are (add whatever label you want), so we cannot fellowship with you." Folks, the world is going to Hell daily. If the Church does not work together for the Lord's good, we will not be effective for the kingdom. I am not asking for an ecumenical movement, but for a movement of grace whereby we can agree on the majors such as the reformation themes—faith alone, Christ alone, and grace alone. That cry helped bring about the Protestant Reformation, and maybe we need a fresh infusion of such thinking today. Then the church would raise the Heavens and the glory of God in such a way that I am convinced Christianity would become more contagious.

Consequence #3

Not only are we hurting ourselves and limiting his glory by not living out grace, we are also hurting others. Grace was never intended to die in us. Grace was intentionally given to flow through us. Why? Because we are more like Christ when we are channels of grace and our grace giving benefits others.

Just think of it in terms of practical application.

1. How many homeless shelters near us would benefit if we gave some time, money, or things?
2. How many university students could be impacted through our time spent on the campus sharing grace with them?
3. How many people out of work could benefit from gift cards to a nearby grocery store for food for their family?
4. How many missionaries come home every year discouraged because of lack of funds or communication from back home?
5. How many lost people live right around us, just waiting for us to extend some grace?
6. How many people have left the church because of an ungracious believer?
7. How many pastors no longer are in the pulpit due to a lack of grace from the leaders? I know of three pastors right near our church who have been forced out of their church by the leadership recently. These are good men who were treated with a lack of grace.

We who have been graced with so much should be the best grace givers on the face of the Earth. Instead, we sometimes forget how much we have been graced. Jesus used a similar picture with his teaching on forgiveness: "For if you forgive men their trespasses, your heavenly Father will also forgive you. But if you do not forgive men their trespasses, neither will your Father forgive your trespasses" (Matt 6:14–15). Then look at the more lengthy passage in Matt 18:21–35 which says,

> Then Peter came to him and said, "Lord, how often shall my brother sin against me, and I forgive him? Up to seven times?"
> Jesus said to him, "I do not say to you, up to seven times, but up to seventy times seven. Therefore the kingdom of heaven is like a certain king who wanted to settle accounts with his servants. And when he had begun to settle accounts, one was brought to him who owed him ten thousand talents. But as he was not able to pay, his master commanded that he be sold, with his wife and children and all that he had, and that payment be made. The servant therefore fell down before him, saying, 'Master, have patience

Benefits of Grace Living

with me, and I will pay you all.' Then the master of that servant was moved with compassion, released him, and forgave him the debt.

"But that servant went out and found one of his fellow servants who owed him a hundred denarii; and he laid hands on him and took *him* by the throat, saying, 'Pay me what you owe!' So his fellow servant fell down at his feet and begged him, saying, 'Have patience with me, and I will pay you all.' And he would not, but went and threw him into prison till he should pay the debt. So when his fellow servants saw what had been done, they were very grieved, and came and told their master all that had been done. Then his master, after he had called him, said to him, 'You wicked servant! I forgave you all that debt because you begged me. Should you not also have had compassion on your fellow servant, just as I had pity on you?' And his master was angry, and delivered him to the torturers until he should pay all that was due to him.

"So My heavenly Father also will do to you if each of you, from his heart, does not forgive his brother his trespasses." (NKJV)

The passage has a great deal of meaning in its entirety, and it is summed up in verse 33, "Should you not also have had compassion on your fellow servant, just as I had pity on you?" Although I don't believe God gives us grace or forgiveness conditioned upon our giving it to others, I believe it is safe to say that it is understood that we should grace others. And why not? After all, we have been graced.

Now let's also run a list here of how our lack of grace toward others personally affects them.

1. They become disillusioned with the church and often fall away.
2. They become bitter toward church and even toward God.
3. They become a poor testimony to the lost community that once knew them to be involved and active.
4. They (especially the children) become confused.

The consequences just continue to roll on. It is like the stone hitting the still waters of a pond; the ripples continue long after the stone has gone. Grace withheld to the believing community does much damage to the picture of the church. But just imagine when God's people are not very gracious to the lost. Do we think it makes them want to seek further what it means to be a follower of Jesus?

Now I certainly have not exhausted the consequences of failing to grace others, but I trust that these are sufficient enough to challenge you about grace. Moreover, let me make one thing clear: we don't grace because we are trying to avoid consequences. We grace because it is our privilege.

Benefits of Grace Living

Benefit #1: It pleases God.

When we act out genuine grace to a world that sees so little of it, you can almost see God's smile. Grace is dear to his heart. He is full of grace and he sent his Son here full of grace. Can you see his radiance as grace circles up towards Heaven as a sweet-smelling aroma like the Old Testament sacrifices that came before him?

We know that Jesus was well pleasing in his sight. He sounded that truth out from Heaven on several occasions while Jesus was on the earth (baptism, transfiguration, and one example in John's Gospel). And we know it is grace living at the foundation of all this. Paul makes that clear in 2 Cor 8:9: "For you know the *grace* of our Lord Jesus Christ, that though He was rich, yet for your sakes He became poor, that you through His poverty might become rich" (emphasis mine). Notice what is obviously placed at the beginning of this verse? Jesus lived out grace and was pleasing in the Father's sight. Do we understand that by living this way we, too, can be well pleasing in his sight? We are that way positionally, but we must also live it practically.

Benefit #2: You cannot out-give God.

When you do something for God, you know that he says, "You cannot give me more blessing than I can give you." Try it and see. God told the same to Israel through the prophet Malachi in 3:10 of his book: "'Bring all the tithes into the storehouse, that there may be food in My house, And try Me now in this,' says the Lord of hosts, 'If I will not open for you the windows of heaven and pour out for you *such* blessing that *there will* not *be room* enough *to receive it*'" (NKJV, emphasis mine). It appears that God is asking us to try him out. God is not going to allow us mere mortals to out-grace him. We can bless and give on a limited level, but he can bless far beyond our imagination.

My wife and I were at a mission's conference and the host brought a list of items for us to pray about/donate to. Neither my wife nor I talked about it at that time, but later we discussed the request and God laid an

Benefits of Grace Living

amount on our hearts. We obeyed the Lord and before the year was over, God had given the amount back in a way we did not even see coming. Now we did not give to test God, but I cannot say I did not wonder about if/how God would bless us through this. God proved faithful in this case and many more times in the lives of his children. Paul says in 2 Cor 9:6–9:

> But this I say: He who sows sparingly will also reap sparingly, and he who sows bountifully will also reap bountifully. So let each one give as he purposes in his heart, not grudgingly or of necessity; for God loves a cheerful giver. And God is able to make all grace abound toward you, that you, always having all sufficiency in all things, may have an abundance for every good work. As it is written: "He has dispersed abroad, He has given to the poor; His righteousness endures forever." (NKJV)

Again, did you notice what word God uses in the midst of this principle? God is able to make all grace abound because he is not willing to allow you to out grace him. We just cannot do it. Now I am sure someone would like to give or bless for the wrong reasons. We give our house to God and expect him to give us a mansion. I am not suggesting that we tempt the Lord, but he has no problem with us trying or testing him. It is far bigger than that.

I have read about many great men and women of the faith who have learned this principle so well. They begin to tithe or donate, and before long their baseline number has increased significantly. They receive such joy through giving and watching God bless. He will not be outdone by our pitiful giving. He takes glory in being the greatest Grace Giver of all. What a joy to watch him at work.

But far too many believers never get the chance to experience this joy because they are too busy counting their coins, or dollars, stocks, or dividends, or whatever. If we learn to seek him first, he will take care of us. While I am not suggesting foolishness, I do strongly promote trusting God to provide when all we have is him.

Here's a possible scenario: say that you save for a year to buy a new washing machine. That is good stewardship, because you don't borrow for depreciating items. You thank God for providing the money to save, and you give him the glory for that. None of that is wrong. But what if, near the end of the year, you suddenly hear about an urgent need? After prayer, you believe God wants you to donate the money you saved toward the washing machine. So you give the money, and just then your old washing machine dies. Suddenly, a knock comes at your door. A neighbor is moving overseas and needs to get rid of his new washing machine and dryer right away. If you hadn't given to that need, God still would have received the glory, but when you did, God's power is highlighted much more. I suspect we often miss these kinds of miracles because we take it upon ourselves to meet our needs instead of sacrificial giving and trusting him.

Benefit #3: Grace living protects us from being consumed by the world.

The world is all about having, keeping, owning, and possessing. "He who dies with the most toys wins" is the all-consuming mentality. As Corrie ten Boom said, "Hold everything in your hands lightly, otherwise it hurts when God pries your fingers open." We need to remember that it all belongs to him in the first place. We are simply stewards of what we have been entrusted. Then why do we hold on to that which is fleeting?

One Sunday morning at our church during the Sunday School hour, one of our dear ladies who loved the Lord injected a comment into our discussion about things and possessions, "It is all going to burn, anyway." Interestingly enough, she was tragically killed in a car accident not many days later. Her words still resonate with us.

Absorbing this lesson, which is also taught in Scripture, helps us to be more of a grace giver and grace liver. These things are not ours. This world is not ours. I have been bought with a price and he owns me and all that he entrusted to me. If he wants something in my care to be given to others, who am I to stand in the way? We need to hold on to this world lightly.

The world sucks us into its mold so easily. We learn to justify our behavior by rationalization and humanistic thinking. We need to be careful to not think like the world. Just because the world does something does not make it right. Don't you find it interesting that Jesus' theology is so countercultural? Take for example these thoughts:

1. You want to be great, serve. The world says it you want to be great, have servants.
2. You want to be first, be last. The world says get to the front of the line.
3. You want to be rich, give away. The world says invest, hoard, save, etc.

God does not want us conformed to this world. He wants us instead to transform this world by living differently. I wonder how do our lives differ from the world's way of thinking. We remember the illustration of the frog and the hot water. If you put a frog into hot water, he will immediately jump out (at least so I have been told). But if you put a frog into regular water and slowly heat it up, he will stay in and die, not recognizing the gradual change. Believers today are so immersed in the world that they are being slowly boiled to death by the world's views. You need to ask—are you a transformer or a conformer?

Benefit #4: Grace living helps us develop contentment.

Contentment is a word that has virtually disappeared from the American language. When was the last time you heard that word in any context at all? We eat too much, and yet we are rarely content with our meal. We have cars that work, but are not new enough, so we have to buy a newer model. We have clothes that fit, but need the newest trend. We have houses that meet our needs, but often buy larger for prestige. Are we not being drawn into the world's way of thinking?

What if we learned contentment? Yes, that dress is old, those shoes are aging, that car has 200,000 miles even if it is still going strong, so God certainly would not mind us buying, would he? I am not suggesting it is wrong to get a new car or new dress. But we are such a throw-away society that we often never ask if God would help us be content with that which may be outdated. We just buy and move on.

I understand how hard it is to be content in today's society, but our quest to keep up with the world has caused the benevolent spirit of believers to diminish. What used to be a typical sacrificial community now is battling the same worries as the world. God does not want us to be foolish, but we also do not want to be conformed to this world with a lack of contentment. For all that is in the world is not of the Father (1 John 2:16).

Grace living says that all we have is a gift from the Lord, whether that gift is outdated or not as nice as the newest thing available. Grace living realizes that we are only here for a short time and are strangers and pilgrims and do not need to be enamored with the world to the point that we fall in love with the world. Grace living helps us rise above being conformed to this world.

I have certainly not exhausted all the benefits of grace living. I would imagine you can list quite a few more. My intent was not to give all that I could imagine because the list is immense. The point is that grace living has its benefits. First and foremost, there is the here and now. We live a grace life and grace living is the path the Lord wants us to travel. But I have not even scratched the surface of grace benefits when we stand before the Lord. Not only can we not out give God, we cannot imagine what awaits those who have learned to live by his grace standards. It will be worth it all when we can lay at his feet the rewards given to us for our obedience as stewards of his grace. Do you want to be a part of that and hear "Well done," or be part of those ashamed. I doubt there will be any in Heaven who will have wished that they had lived more for self on that day!

One of the responsibilities of pastors is visiting those in hospitals. Over the years I have sat by many bedsides and heard many last words of believers. One thing that I have never heard from anyone is the wish that they had been more selfish or me-centered. It is sometimes sad to hear the stories of the many who wish they had done more for the Kingdom. Don't wait for that day. Let grace flow out and watch God in action as he takes his grace entrusted to us and feeds the multitudes. It only takes a willing boy with a small lunch to see God do great things.

CHAPTER 9

Be a Difference Maker

Accountability

AT SOME POINT ON the Christian journey, every believer has to pause and ask some hard questions about his or her life. We have "only one life, 'twill soon be past. Only what's done for Christ will last." What are you doing that makes any difference?

I turned 60 this past year, and when I was a child, 60 seemed very old indeed! Now that I am there, it does not seem as old. I guess it is all relative. But one thing is for sure—it goes by fast. The words of the Apostle James rings so true, "Life is a vapor" (Jas 4:14). When I was little, I remember waiting for summer, or my birthday, or Christmas and wondering whether it would ever get here. Time does not seem to be the same today as it was then. I often wish that I could slow things down so that I can get everything done on time.

Every day, I am reminded that life and time wait for no one. Soon we will all stand before the judgment seat of Christ and will have to give account of our lives. Far too often I hear believers say that they are going to do something for Christ "someday." When they are in college, it will happen when they graduate. When they are just married, as soon as the "adjustment period" is over. Once the kids are born, the new parents need to cultivate those early years so that they are not wounded or scarred. Then come school, sports, and preparing them for college. Once the kids are in college, we need to work more to just pay for their tuition. Now we are planning for a wedding or grandkids or whatever. It seems that the time to sacrifice for Kingdom business is always another day than the present. What is sad is that for some believers, that day never comes.

Then we die and stand before the Lord and give account of our lives. Do we think that, with all we have been entrusted, there will not be a day of reckoning? Do we think that our Savior who sacrificed all for us will not hold us to some level of sacrifice and surrender to his will?

Let's be reminded of that day of accountability from the words of Scripture (all references in this section from NKJV):

1. "But why do you judge your brother? Or why do you show contempt for your brother? For we shall all stand before the judgment seat of Christ" (Rom 14:10). Now what does that mean? Every believer will stand before the judgment seat of Christ. No one will be exempt. Also, Rom 14:12 says that we will be required to give account. There is such an effort today to do away with any kind of accountability for the believer. There is even a concerted effort to do away with a literal, burning, eternal Hell. It really does not matter what we *think* Scripture says or what we *want* Scripture to say. The only issue is what Scripture says. It is clear—we are going to give account and we can be sure that accountability will be connected to what we have been entrusted. Grace does not mean no accountability.

2. Paul's words in 1 Cor 3:9–14 should be sober reminders that God takes what we have been given seriously:

   > For we are God's fellow workers; you are God's field, *you are* God's building. According to the grace of God which was given to me, as a wise master builder I have laid the foundation, and another builds on it. But let each one take heed how he builds on it. For no other foundation can anyone lay than that which is laid, which is Jesus Christ. Now if anyone builds on this foundation *with* gold, silver, precious stones, wood, hay, straw, each one's work will become clear; for the Day will declare it, because it will be revealed by fire; and the fire will test each one's work, of what sort it is. If anyone's work which he has built on *it* endures, he will receive a reward. If anyone's work is burned, he will suffer loss; but he himself will be saved, yet so as through fire.

3. In 2 Cor 5:10, Paul admonishes his readers, "For we must all appear before the judgment seat of Christ, that each one may receive the

things *done* in the body, according to what he has done, whether good or bad." On that day, Jesus will evaluate our lives and determine what we have done with the things with which we have been entrusted. We will not be judged for sin (as was discussed earlier), but for our lives as believers. How have we handled his grace? Some believers will be ashamed at that day, and there are even "believers" who are not going to make that day because they professed but did not possess (Matt 7:21–23).

Now once we have had that day of accountability, Scripture adds that we will be given crowns that represent our service for him. There are at least five crowns that are mentioned in the New Testament that will be given on that day. I am not confident that these are the only five that will be shared, but they offer an interesting foretaste of the rewards that await us.

Crown 1: 1 Corinthians 9:25—incorruptible crown

Crown 2: 1 Thessalonians 2:19—rejoicing crown

Crown 3: 2 Timothy 4:8—righteous crown

Crown 4: James 1:12—life crown

Crown 5: 1 Peter 5:4—glory crown

What is equally interesting is that the word for *crown* is the same word that describes the crown that was on our Lord's head. He took the crown of pain for us so we could have the crowns of rewards on that day. Only our Savior would do such a thing for us! But then we get to take those crowns and cast them at his feet. What a day that will be! Read Rev 4–5 and get a fresh picture of that day. The believer ought to desire to be as fully rewarded as possible on that day, to worship him on the highest level possible. What have we done with our grace gifts?

And it does not stop there. We return with our Lord to help set up the Kingdom on earth and will be rewarded there as well with privileges of service for his 1000-year reign on the earth (2 Tim 2:12 and Rev 3:21). I suspect that Heaven also will have privileges based on how we have handled our giftedness. Shouldn't there be a desire in all of us to give all we have and serve to the fullest?

The Needs are Great

Our Lord made a strong statement about the needs and the workers as recorded in Matt 9:37–38: "Then He said to His disciples, "The harvest is plentiful, but the laborers are few. Therefore, pray to the Lord of the harvest to send out laborers into His harvest." Here, two points are driven home. First, the harvest (people and their lives) is great. Second, those who are willing to tend to the needs are few. In other words, we have enough Christians working in the secular world. We need those who are willing to do Kingdom business. Now let me clarify. I am not saying that you cannot be a mechanic, dentist, factory worker, or any other career out there. But if you think that it accounts for what Jesus is discussing in Matt 9, then you are greatly mistaken. Can ministry occur at work? Absolutely. Is it? You can answer that for yourself. Few are making any kind of difference in the workplace. You may be the exception, but over the years, all I hear is, "It's a job. I'm just putting in time for a paycheck." We have divided the sacred and secular, but nowhere in Scripture does God do so.

How many today are graduating from high school or college and heading into full-time ministry of any sort? The average age of missionaries gets older every year, and few are following in their steps. Yet the needs continue to grow.

Let me review some statistics from earlier. These are from World Hunger:[1]

1. 1.5 million children die every year from hunger
2. 33% of world population considered to be starving
3. 3.6 seconds is the time between deaths of those dying from hunger
4. 800 million is the number of people suffering from hunger and malnutrition
5. 936 million people don't have enough to eat
6. 98% of people in developing nations have enough to eat
7. 20,864 people died today of hunger
8. 7,615,360 people will die of hunger this year
9. 11% of US households are at risk of hunger

---

1. "World Hunger Statistics." *Statistic Brain RSS*. N.p., n.d. Web. 1 Oct. 2014.

Be a Difference Maker

Jeff Shinabarger, in his book, *More or Less*, did a project that convicted me when I read about it. He and his wife decided to not go to the grocery store again until they ate up all the food that they had on their shelves and refrigerator and freezer. He said that they did have to buy milk and bread and other things that have a short life span. But when the project was completed, they had enough to eat for seven weeks. Now he went on to say that some meals were limited, but he also commented that they did not have a large freezer and overflowing food pantry. It was very simple, yet he could eat for almost two months. I doubt he is alone in our "blessed" nation. But does it bother us that we have two months' worth of sustenance and some of our brothers and sisters in Haiti or Nigeria or some other poor country may go to bed tonight with no food at all?

But there is also the problem of water. According to the World Water Council:[2]

1. 1.1 billion people live without clean drinking water.
2. 2.4 billion people lack adequate sanitation.
3. Water is implicated in 80% of all sickness and disease worldwide.
4. 900 children die every day from water-borne diseases.
5. By the time you read this book, several hundred more will have died.

According to the Water Information Program, Americans use 3.9 trillion gallons of water per month. The average American uses 176 gallons of water per day compared to 5 gallons of water in an average African home.[3] We flush more good water down the toilet in a day than some families have in weeks. By no means is this intended to cause us guilt or despair, rather it should inform us. We need to know these things if we are ever going to be able to effectively pray and discern God's will.

Let's add a further insight to these concerns. There is an area of the world that missionary statesmen have called the 10/40 Window. It is the area that lies across Africa and Asia from 10 degrees latitude north of the equator to 40 degrees latitude north of the equator. Within that area lives two-thirds of the world's population, roughly 4.4 billion people. 90 percent of these people are un-evangelized. Many have never heard the Gospel message one time. There are either no believers or not enough believers in

---

2. "Water Crisis." World Water Council. Accessed October 1, 2014.

3. "The Water Information Program | Providing Water Information to the Communities of Southwest Colorado." Accessed October 1, 2014. http://www.waterinfo.org.

many areas of the 10/40 Window to even make any evangelical impact.[4] How shall they hear without a preacher? The only way these people are going to hear is if someone leaves their culture and goes to theirs to reach them. It is part of the Great Commission.

This type of statistic does not appear in most pulpit messages. We are too busy chasing the American dream and doing whatever that we have no time or energy for the world. We are putting our hands over our eyes, over our ears and sticking our heads into the sand as if that will keep us from knowing. We are like the kid at bedtime who thinks the "boogey man" is in our room so we pull the blanket over our head and hope for the best. The American church has curled up in a fetal position and pulled the covers over its head and is willing to keep on going without knowing or caring. Maybe we are too busy building our own kingdom to be truly immersed into building his? Maybe we are too pulled by the world to be able to impact the world? Maybe we are just too American in thought to handle Biblical concepts? Well, that won't make any of these things go away. Nor can we go to Pilate's bowl and wash our hands of the weight of the world. The needs of our brothers and sisters all over are just as much our needs as those of the brothers or sisters who sit next to us every Sunday morning. Yes, ministering to the needs of our global family is costly, but if not us, who?

If you realize the physical needs are great, put in perspective the spiritual needs. There are an estimated 7.5 billion people on the earth. Roughly 40 percent of them have not even been reached with the Gospel. Now, I am not saying that 60 percent are believers, but just that 60 percent at least have been communicated with on some level. Please do not think this is good news. I cannot tell you how many times we have heard stories, even in our own country, where the Gospel has no impact. On one occasion when a child evangelism worker was sharing the truth of Jesus to an inner city group, one child ran home and told her mom that some lady was swearing at them. When the mom came to investigate, she found out the swear word was the name "Jesus" that was being shared with them by way of the Gospel.

If you add the "heard-but-not-received" group to our calculations, the total number of unreached people in the world seems to grow to significantly more than 60 percent. If one out of seven people is a believer, for example, that would mean that 6 billion people are headed for hell. Does that concern you at all?

---

4. "What Is the 10/40 Window? :: Joshua Project." Accessed September 12, 2014.

Be a Difference Maker

I once heard a story that was staggering. I was sitting in a college chapel service and the man said he had three truths to share in closing. Truth 1: Every 3 seconds someone dies in the world and goes to Hell. Truth 2: Most of us don't give a d— (and yes, this was a Christian college campus). Truth 3: The majority of us are more upset about truth 2 than about truth 1. Ouch. He was right. He then went on to explain the word "damn" in a Biblical context with damnation. It was intriguing, but regardless, the point was driven home. I, too, was guilty. Are you?

Yes, we must agree that the needs are great, both physically and spiritually. If you don't see it as your responsibility, I ask you . . . whose responsibility is it? Of course, we don't have to meet *every* need just because there is a need. That is not what I am saying. But to ignore all the needs, do very little, if anything at all, and instead allow yourself to be consumed with this world truly is not right either. The needs at least ought to cause us to seek His face and attempt to determine what he would have us to do.

Just one example might help us see this somewhat clearer. First, a few personal thoughts. I have been thrilled as a parent to raise children who enjoy sports. At an early age, we put our children in the local sport's programs and began the journey of sports and travel and even coaching. It was truly an enjoyable adventure. But one thing I noticed as the time went on was how often sports began to be in conflict with the Lord's work. Sunday activities used to be minimal, but now they have become the norm. Then the family, with practices and games and travel and expense, has little left over for the Lord's work. I struggle to believe that when we stand before God he is going to be most concerned about our AAU statistics or Little League batting average. With all the needs around us, is there not a balance?

How can I make a difference?

I am just one person. How can I make a difference? 4.4 billion people is far out of my reasonable reach. I can't provide water to all those thirsty children. I could not give all my money and even make a dent into this need.

If you remember the title of the book, you will notice that I have given it a title that in some ways is not grammatically correct. *Graced 2 Grace* is really not proper English. But, there is a reason I have given it this title. The "2" does refer to the actual number 2. Why have I done it this way? Because it takes two.

In order to understand this better, try to remember the Biblical stories of God doing amazing things through unlikely and often ill-equipped people. Noah, as one man, saved the world. Abraham became the Father of the Hebrew nation. Moses led the people out of Egypt to the Promised Land. David took down the giant with one small stone. The little boy donated his lunch and fed 5,000. It took only two: God is always ready to do his part; it is just that the laborers are few.

I wonder if we have lost sight of the power of our God. We far too often look at our resources and conclude that something is not possible. It is not possible for one small lunch to feed 5,000. That is true. But, if we see grace as we should, then that is something that is within our reach. God loves to take the small amount that we can offer and do a great miracle so that when all is said and done, no one can get the glory but him. He will not share his glory with another. If we can do great things and then give a seminar or write a book on it and explain how it all happened, then we have to wonder whether God had anything to do with it at all.

First Corinthians 1:26–31 ought to be our motto. Let me share that passage with you in its entirety:

> For you see your calling, brethren, that not many wise according to the flesh, not many mighty, not many noble, *are called*. But God has chosen the foolish things of the world to put to shame the wise, and God has chosen the weak things of the world to put to shame the things which are mighty; and the base things of the world and the things which are despised God has chosen, and the things which are not, to bring to nothing the things that are, that no flesh should glory in His presence. But of him you are in Christ Jesus, who became for us wisdom from God—and righteousness and sanctification and redemption—that, as it is written, "He who glories, let him glory in the Lord."

Unfortunately what happens most frequently in the believing community is we become grace absorbers and not difference makers. We have seen his grace and embraced his grace and have concluded that this grace is for us to enjoy this earth more. Isn't it possible that an attitude like this is more reflective of a lost man than a believer? Maybe those who profess to be followers are truly not even followers at all.

Over my years as a pastor, I have met so many wonderful God-fearing people who truly are making a difference with their lives. Let me give a few references and details of some of those that I have personally encountered.

My former associate pastor, Marvin Patrick, and his wife, Debbie, are two such examples. They have been at the church during my entire tenure and just recently left for Marvin to pursue a call to minister as a senior pastor which, in turn, has led them to become church planters. This couple could easily have just sat back and drifted for their last few years of ministry. They had a ministry, home, family, friends, and the respect of the community. But the call of God was too great, and they ventured out like Abraham looking for a place of God's choosing. They want to be difference makers. I can't wait to see how he is going to use them.

My associate pastor, Keith Surland, is also quite an example to me. He had a lucrative career in furniture refinishing but sensed a call to full-time ministry. He went on to seminary and did his internship at our church. It was our first encounter with him. After his internship, we invited him to join us for full-time ministry and he has not stopped since. God has gifted this man greatly and he is presently leading door-to-door evangelism, Greek classes, and Bible studies. He has made numerous trips to the Ukraine reaching the unsaved in small villages. His lasting impact will be a joy to observe. He is a difference maker.

I hesitate to add this third one, but I believe with all my heart that she is one of the most amazing difference makers that I know. I am referring to my wife. About 20 years ago, she, being a senior pastor's wife and mother of four, volunteered her time to help our struggling Christian school. She was already buried in diapers and mothering, not counting trying to minister to me (which is her biggest challenge). One year she cleaned all the school bathrooms because we could not afford a janitor. For several years she worked with no pay. She became the face of the Christian school. This past year she retired (although too young), to focus on a different ministry. This year we go to Brazil and next year to India. But the school has impacted many lives and only eternity will reveal the lasting impact of this difference maker.

These are just a few examples of difference makers that I know personally. There are many more, but I wanted to at least give you a taste of the difference maker potential. I recently met with a family who gave all kinds of excuses as to why they could not be involved in ministry at this time. They had small children, he worked long hours, they were too young in the faith, etc. I challenged them to consider being a difference maker now. We don't know how long we have. This might be our last day on the earth and we are consumed by our needs and our wishes and our wants while many go hurting and unreached. Yes, we cannot meet all the needs, but my greatest burden and concern is that many believers they just don't care. Apathy is the typical response today.

But if not me, then who? Why is it always someone else who is expected to be a difference maker? We know the world has needs both physically and spiritually. We know that we have been blessed. We know (especially after reading this book) that we have blessed to bless (graced to grace). So, what are we waiting for? Put the book down and do something. In fact, in the next sections I offer some suggestions to help you know what "something" you should do.

Before Becoming a Difference Maker

In order to be a difference maker for the King, we have to be confident that we are truly one of his followers. Far too many are attempting to walk with the Lord and have no true personal relationship with him. There ought to be clear evidences that we are a child of God.

2 Corinthians 5:17 says, "Therefore, if anyone *is* in Christ, *he is* a new creation; old things have passed away; behold, all things have become new." The Greek makes is clear that if you say you are in Christ, old things are gone (sinful habits and ways), and all things are in the process of becoming new. We are not immediately perfect. We still fall short. But there needs to be specific change in our lives if we truly born again. If there has never been a time where you were born again and there was clear and obvious change, then maybe you are not a follower at all? It is worth taking a serious look at this truth and making sure you are in the faith. You ought to know it to be true (1 John 5:13).

If you have this confidence that you are a child of God and fruit to back it up (John 15:8), then it is time go on and make a difference in this world. I cannot tell you how many funerals I have observed where the family goes on and on about their great dad or mom or grandparent. I personally stopped doing eulogies years ago because the families often expected me to say great things about their departed love one. I am not trying to be unkind here, but if they taught you to cook, fish, hunt, golf, sports, read, or whatever, so what? We hear at funeral after funeral about someone's amazing dad or mom, and yet there is little or no spiritual discussion mentioned. Again (not trying to be harsh), if the finality of our lives is measured by earthly standards only, have we not wasted an entire life and the great depth of grace with which we have been entrusted?

Be a Difference Maker

This is not our world. We are here simply as guests of God and our calling is to make an impact for him. In this is our Father glorified as we bear much fruit, so says Jesus. Our lives ought to be consumed by him and his call on our journey. If not, then what is life all about?

So, in order to be a difference maker two things needs to be clear. First, there needs to be obvious and clear evidence that you are God's child. Second, you must make his calling your consumption. David Platt's book calls this sold-out-to-Jesus mindset "radical." While that's quite true in our culture, it's sad that it must be considered radical. Jesus would call it Christian.

The Specifics of Being a Difference Maker

So, how do we truly live out grace in this world today? What path should a believe take to grace others with the grace entrusted to him? I will make a few suggests, but please not limit this to an exact checklist. Instead, see this as a model for prayer and serious contemplation in the presence of God. God graced us to use us. So let's get on with gracing others with our grace. Here is a suggested list.

Suggestion 1: In order to effectively grace others, we need a life of prayer.

It begins with a life of prayer. Researchers today all confirm that prayerlessness is a major concern in the body of Christ. Some research has concluded that even pastors' prayer lives are minimal. One such survey suggests that the average parishioner prays less than three minutes a day and the average pastor less than five minutes a day. If this is even close to accurate, how can we even believe we are in touch with our Father who owns this world and determines all things according to his counsel? Can you imagine a married couple spending three to five minutes a day with each other and having a fruitful and effective marriage? It is not going to happen. Neither can a believer and God have an effective relationship in doing the will of the Father when there is not deep and continuous prayer life. It begins here. We can only be effective gracing others with this grace if we have a life of conversation with our Father that enables us to have a daily walk and receive our daily marching orders.

Prayer is almost like having a job where the employees meet in the morning to map out the strategy for the day. There is the closed-door meeting, and the head of the business explains the daily tasks. Prayer works in a similar way for us. Yes, we have a general directive from God, but daily we need to be sure that not only are we hearing from him, but that something is not hindering his whispers to our heart. Oh, that each of us would have a meeting early every day with God where he speaks clearly to us through his Word and prayer, and we head out the door not to be a part of the world, but to be an ambassador for the King of the world!

I suggest that we need to become world-class pray-ers. Since believers in China and Russia and Chile are our brothers and sisters, their burdens are our burdens. It would be wise for us to become more involved with missionaries all over the world. We need a prayer list of their requests and we must pray over those requests as fervently as we do over those for our immediate family. Overall, missionaries have little support from the local church. We put them in front when they come through on furlough, but how serious are we regarding their mission work? I am confident that we don't share their burdens deeply enough or we would think and live with a missional mindset. How would we even know whether God wants us to go on a short-term trip to the mission field if we really have no heart connection?

Our church publishes a monthly prayer journal where the overall missionary letters are streamlined so we can pray a reasonable list of prayer requests. We also send the entire newsletter around to whoever would want to see all the requests. We desire to have prayers going up for all the missionaries we support. In doing so, people begin to connect. It is amazing just how prayer works in this manner. And it just cannot be a periodic prayer life. When Scripture says we are to pray without ceasing, it is more than just a command (1 Thess 5:17). I believe Paul is suggesting that we need a walk of prayer. Our life ought to be an ongoing prayer. As David prayed morning, noon, and night, so we also need to be in daily and regular contact with our Father. This is not an option if we are going to be a world-class Christian.

Suggestion 2: In order to effectively grace others, we need to be a student of Scripture.

Today's church is Biblically deficient. I am not suggesting we could not answer questions on Jeopardy, but the Word is not impacting our daily lives. As was said long ago in a song I once heard: "I hear you are getting into the

Word, but is the Word getting into you?" We need to be reminded of what 2 Tim 2:15 says, "Be diligent to present yourself approved to God, a worker who does not need to be ashamed, rightly dividing the word of truth." This verse suggests serious study. I am not talking about morning devotions or daily crumbs. I am talking about diligent, studious handling of Scripture.

Muslims are taught to memorize the Koran, and many children do so at an early age. They know their book inside and out. Can we be any less serious? It is shocking to see how many professing Christians there are that never regularly study God's Word. They attend churches that offer soft messages that rarely handle the Word of God, they are part of no serious Bible study, and they personally invest very little into God's Word. Have you ever stopped to ponder why the Bible was given to us? It was given to us so that we could get to know our God. The Unknowable God has revealed himself to us so that we can know him (Phil 3:10). Careful diligence and time ought to be devoted to his Word so we can truly know him and know what he expects of us. Instead, we are comfortable with only the *One Minute Bible* and the moments of contemplation. I have never met a difference maker who was not a serious student of the Word of God.

If you spend 15 minutes a day in Bible study, you have given to the Lord roughly one percent of your day. There are 96 periods of 15 minutes each day. How can anyone believe that they are devoted to the Word when so little time is invested? We spend more time in line at Starbucks that we do in the Bible. Being a difference maker starts with the Word and prayer.

Suggestion 3: In order to effectively grace others, we need to be a world-class Christian.

Of course, this is related to being a world-class pray-er that I discussed above. I recently read the book entitled *How to Be a World-Class Christian* by Paul Borthwick. It was eye-opening and convicting, and after reading it, I concluded that I had much to improve in order to reach that goal. Basically, a world-class Christian is a believer who sees the world as their call. Scripture supports such a claim:

- John 3:16—God so loved the world . . .
- Matthew 28:19–20—Go into all the world . . .
- Acts 1:8—Go into the uttermost parts of the world . . .

Believers who choose to limit their view of the needs of the world and their responsibility are never going to be difference makers. Instead, they are going to brighten the corner where they are and put their hands over their eyes to the rest of the needs of the world. Can we honestly believe that such a perspective makes an impact?

Some people may feel that they can do very little. They may have deep limitations such as health, finances, or debilitating demands. Let me remind you not to limit God. We have been told to impact the world, so let's do so by faith. God is not going to call you to do something that cannot be done. Remember the boy and his lunch? The little you offer may be just what Jesus will use to spread his Word to unbelievers. Begin to step out in faith.

Start looking for ways to stretch yourself. Consider soft steps first with rescue missions, or crisis pregnancy centers, or homeless shelters. Then begin to branch out from there to include ministries just outside of your personal scope. We have connected with an inner-city church and are attempting to assist them as they impact their community. In addition, there are ministries in very rural areas that are so primitive it would amaze you. Some of those in very remote sections of our country have very little. Once you have begun to reach out from a short radius around your church, you could begin to pray for God to take you to a cross-cultural ministry. There are missionaries all over the world that would love to have a family visit and support their work for a week or two. It could make lasting impacts on you, them, and the mission field that literally bears eternal fruit.

To this day, God is still using some short-term mission trips in my life in ways that I would never have believed. I can still see the families, the lost, the homeless, the hurting, and the needy in front of my eyes. I am not the same because of the trips taken overseas for his glory. They humble me and break me every time, all of which are greatly needed. Thank you, Lord.

Suggestion 4: In order to effectively grace others, we need to have a sacrificial heart.

We discussed earlier that few believers have a sacrificial mindset. We live in such a materialistic world that we have little burden for the hurting and little concern to do anything about it. Try to be honest here, do you have a sacrificial heart? How have you sacrificed for the Kingdom in the last five years, in the last year, in the last month, or even the last week?

Here is how we typically define sacrifice. I serve in the church. I make meals for those who are in need. I shoveled someone's driveway when they could not. I gave some clothes to the homeless.

I remember when we were going through this series at church and a mom came up to me after the message. She wanted to share a story about her son. She wanted to show me that even children could get the message. We had announced a few weeks earlier that a nearby home had been destroyed by fire and they had lost everything. We shared the ages of the children and asked if anyone could assist. This was not a family from our church. This little boy had just celebrated a birthday and had some new toys. He wanted to share his brand-new toys with this family, not the old ones he did not play with. This little boy got it. He understood sacrifice.

Our Lord modeled this for us as well. He left the splendor of Heaven, took up flesh, became a servant, and died a criminal death. I love how Mark records it for us in Mark 10:43-45: "Yet it shall not be so among you; but whoever desires to become great among you shall be your servant. And whoever of you desires to be first shall be slave of all. For even the Son of Man did not come to be served, but to serve, and to give His life a ransom for many."

Could it be any clearer? Our life on this earth is not about our comfort, our glory, our pleasure, our joy, our wants, our desires, our whatever. Our life on this earth is about him and his glory. And if you think that living godly means you get all the world's goods and comforts as well as the spiritual blessings, you need to travel to the huts in Haiti, and the high rises in Russia, and the impoverished in India and discover some of the most godly people you will ever meet and realize that godliness does not mean you are going to have earthly treasures. Godliness does not necessarily equal comfort. As a matter of fact, Scripture implies the opposite. Second Timothy 3:12 states: "Yes, and all who desire to live godly in Christ Jesus will suffer persecution." I wonder if maybe American godliness and Biblical godliness are different.

This is where asking God for a sacrificial heart could benefit us. A person with a sacrificial heart is a person who sees that they own nothing, but are mere stewards of the grace of God. Therefore, God has the sovereign right to take what he has entrusted to us and use it for his glory at any time. This person simply manages these grace gifts and looks for his leading for how he wants these gifts used for his glory. May God help us to see this through his eyes.

Suggestion 5: In order to effectively grace others, we need to fall in love with the church.

It greatly saddens me today to see how believers have fallen away from the local church. I understand that church leaders have messed up at times. But the church is all about Christ. We need to keep our eyes on him and realize that the church is the best plan to reach the world for Christ. Now I realize that there are parachurch organizations that are doing great works for God. But in order to really be effective and to make the most impact, all kingdom business ought to run through the local church and under the local church. Christ has promised to build his church and protect it and use it for Kingdom work. We need to make the local church the priority it ought to be.

Here are the steps:

1. Find a Bible-believing church and commit to it. What is a Bible-believing church? One that holds to the fundamentals of the faith such as inspiration of Scripture, Deity of Jesus Christ, Trinity, and other similar historic doctrines. This church not only should believe these truths, but it should teach and preach them regularly.

2. Get involved seriously with this church. That means understanding your spiritual gift and serving our King for his glory. You ought to be attending regularly. In other words, people should not be shocked to see you at church, but shocked when you are not there. You ought to conspicuous by your presence.

3. Speak well of your local church. Bad mouthing only does harm to the Kingdom plan. Yes, there are problems at every local church level. If you find a church with no problems, please do not join it and mess it up! Problems are part of people and the church contains people. Let the community and your family and workplace hear only of the blessings of the church where you are planted.

4. Guard your criticism of the shepherds. Believers who tear down and wear down the leadership do more damage than they will ever realize. I have been both a parishioner and a pastor. I have seen both sides rather clearly. Your criticism of the church leadership is doing serious damage to the cause of Christ. Is there a place for criticism? Yes, but it needs to be guarded well. Let me offer a few thoughts about handling the desire to be critical.

a. Trust God to oversee his church. It is not your responsibility. God does it better than you ever will. Let him be the Head as he can so effectively do. I suspect sometimes our interference hinders him dealing with leadership properly.

b. Trust your pastor. He is a gifted man to the local church (Eph 4:11–16). God can work through him, but if you continue to criticize him, he may become ineffective and that is on you. Let me give an example of how this works via a marriage. A wife thinks she is helping her family by being critical of dad behind his back ("I'm just showing them that he's not as perfect as they think he is.") What she is doing instead is undermining the authority path and actually drawing hardship to herself. The children will learn to disrespect her in the process. A critical spirit aimed at the pastor will hurt you and hinder Kingdom work. As a pastor, I can tell the families that are critical of me behind my back by how their children treat me. Almost without exception, a home that does not support the pastor will be evidenced by the children's lack of support and respect. And we wonder why our children are pulling away from the church.

c. Realize that to criticize the man of God can be an attack on God's anointed. I want to tread lightly here, but it is a truth that needs to be taught. God puts pastors in leadership by his sovereign choosing. A critical spirit that is destructive can bring harm to you personally. David was grieved in his heart to simply tear a part of King Saul's clothing, and Saul was a godless man. How much caution should there be towards a God-fearing man. This doesn't mean we should let pastors get away with anything, but we should be very, very cautious. First Timothy 5:19 says we are not even to receive an accusation without witnesses. Be cautious here.

5. Do all you can to bring others to Christ and help build the local church. Go about it with fever and passion. Be sold out to this cause because it is the one God has clearly chosen to put his hands on. It is his church that will change the world. If you want to be a part of that, then the local church is your avenue.

Somewhere along the way each of us have to ask seriously the eternal questions of our existence. How do you want your life to matter in this world? How do you want to live your life out in view of his glory? If you are being a difference maker already, keep on keeping on. Ask God if he wants you to increase your work.

If you stay on the path you presently are on, what difference are you going to make? Maybe it is time you just do something?

CHAPTER 10

Concluding Thoughts

WE HAVE BEEN GRACED to grace. When we realize that everything—the air we breathe, the material blessings we enjoy, and the oh-so-great salvation—are all gifts from God, our mindset goes from "me" to "he." He, the great Creator of the universe, has given each and every one of us, limited mortals that we are, these gifts with which to grace others. And those others have gifts with which they can grace us. We have seen how we can make a difference, no matter how large or small we perceive God's grace gifts to be. And we know that there is no joy like the joy of spreading God's grace to our brothers and sisters in Christ and from there to a lost and dying world.

But how does it come? Matt Redman, a singer-songwriter of our era, has written many wonderful and moving songs that bring such worship in focus. Some of them are: "10,000 Reasons," "Blessed Be Your Name," and "Your Love Never Fails." But the one that has most moved me might be his recent one entitled: "Your Grace Finds Me."[1] I would suggest if you have never heard this song, listen to it on the Internet and especially note the lyrics. Due to copyright laws I can only give you a sampling, so here goes:

> From the creation to the cross
> There from the cross into eternity
> Your grace finds me ...

---

1. "Your Grace Finds Me" Lyrics. Matt Redman Lyrics. Accessed September 17, 2014.

This song reminds us that we don't have to hunt down God's grace. We may have to open our eyes to recognize it, but it finds us. We, who deserve nothing, receive by the grace of God his unmerited favor. With that we get the privilege to be spent for him for his glory. It just does not get any better than this.

We should walk softly in that grace. Whenever our focus turns inward, we must redirect it upward. The grace doesn't come from inside us, it comes from him. So if we are trying to generate it in our own power, we won't be very successful. It would be like the wind turbines that dot many of the states in the Midwest: they cannot generate any power at all unless the wind is blowing. It's only as his Spirit fills our lives with his life-giving grace that we can spread the power to others. Jesus puts it another way: "I am the vine, you *are* the branches. He who abides in Me, and I in him, bears much fruit; for without Me you can do nothing" (John 15:5, NKJV). We don't want to get to Heaven and have regrets, or say "If I had only . . . " Perhaps you have said that already in your Christian walk when you have failed to let the grace of God overflow in your life. But while you cannot fix the past, you can truly by his grace begin afresh today for the future.

Will you join with me on this journey of Graced 2 Grace? From the cradle to the grave, may your life be a testimony of the grace of God and may your impact be fruit for his pleasure.

APPENDIX 1

Grace Throughout The New Testament

THIS SECTION OFFERS A study I did on the subject of grace. I offer it here so the reader may see the enormous information on grace in the New Testament. I would encourage you to examine the contexts on your own and do your own study of the examples. What is being offered in the next few pages is simply an effort to reduce the plethora of verses on grace to a more manageable number. Some of the examples in the New Testament of grace are actually repeats of other passages. For example: two times in the New Testament does it say that God resists the proud but gives grace to the humble (Jas 4:6 and 1 Pet 5:5). Two passages also teach that we are justified by grace (Rom 3:24 and Tit 3:7). Additionally, not all examples of the word *grace* fit our study. I used these guiding principles to bring number of grace examples to a more palatable list.

These examples hopefully will help jumpstart your own research and give you more tools to bring all glory to the God of all grace.

1. Grace living—Acts 2:47

2. Grace sharing—Acts 4:32-34

3. Grace observing—Acts 11:23 (it is to be seen in us), Galatians 2:9

4. Grace witnessing—Acts 14:3

5. Grace testifying—Acts 20:24

6. Grace justifying—Romans 3:24, Titus 3:7

Grace Throughout The New Testament

7. Grace standing—Romans 5:2, 1 Peter 5:12
8. Grace reigning—Romans 5:17, 21
9. Grace abounding—Romans 5:20, 2 Corinthians 8:7
10. Grace freeing—Romans 6:14-15
11. Grace humbling—Romans 12:3
12. Grace serving—Romans 12:6, Ephesians 3:7, Hebrews 12:28
13. Grace building—1 Corinthians 3:10
14. Grace partaking—1 Corinthians 10:30—our liberty
15. Grace existing—1 Corinthians 15:10
16. Grace victory—1 Corinthians 15:57
17. Grace tithing—1 Corinthians 16:3 (liberality), 2 Corinthians 8:1
18. Grace behaving—2 Corinthians1:12
19. Grace fellowshipping—2 Corinthians 1:15
20. Grace smelling—2 Corinthians 2:14 (as unto the Lord)
21. Grace glorying—2 Corinthians 4:15, 2 Thessalonians 1:12
22. Grace wasting—2 Corinthians 6:1 (what a shame)
23. Grace receiving—2 Corinthians 8:4, 6
24. Grace sacrificing—2 Corinthians 8:9 (example of Jesus), Hebrews 2:9
25. Grace sufficiency—2 Corinthians9:8
26. Grace attracting—2 Corinthians 9:14
27. Grace absorbing—2 Corinthians 12:9
28. Grace leaving—Galatians1:6, 5:4; Hebrews 12:15 (fallen from grace)
29. Grace calling—Galatians1:15; 2 Timothy 1:9
30. Grace measuring—Ephesians 1:7 (riches)
31. Grace ongoing—Ephesians 2:7, 1 Peter 1:13 (more to come)
32. Grace saving—Ephesians 2:9
33. Grace preaching—Ephesians 3:8
34. Grace including (all)—Ephesians 4:7
35. Grace talking—Ephesians 4:25, Colossians 4:6

Grace Throughout The New Testament

36. Grace singing—Colossians 3:16
37. Grace hoping—2 Thessalonians 2:16
38. Grace strengthening—2 Timothy 2:1
39. Grace appearing—Titus 2:11
40. Grace refreshing—Philemon 7 (joy)
41. Grace praying—Hebrews 4:16
42. Grace establishing—Hebrews 13:9
43. Grace preventing –James 4:6, 1 Peter 5:5
44. Grace prophesying—1 Peter 1:10
45. Grace suffering—1 Peter 2:19-20 (thankworthy)
46. Grace inheriting—1 Peter 3:7
47. Grace stewarding—1 Peter 4:10
48. Grace perfecting—1 Peter 5:10
49. Grace growing—2 Peter 5:10
50. Grace turning—Jude 4 (not a good path)

I humbly apologize for any references that I missed that should have been included in our list. The last thing that I would want to do is limit grace. Grace is our all-encompassing picture of our Savior and the privilege we have to walk worthy of our calling.

APPENDIX 2

One-Another Ministry

GRACING ONE ANOTHER MEANS living and serving with each other in many ways. Some ways, of course, are things that we are aware of on a daily basis. Other things may not come to mind right away. Below are 30 biblical references to help you really consider how one-another ministry should take place. I pray that you will contemplate these as you continually strive to pour His grace from your life into others.

There are 25 with positive connotations:

1. Mark 9:50—have peace with one another
2. John 13:14- wash one another's feet
3. John 13:34 (2 times)—love one another, also in 13:35, 15:12, 17; Rom 13:8; 1 Thess 3:12, 4:9; 1 Pet1:22; I Jn 3:11, 23, 4:7, 11, 12; 2 Jn 5 for a total of 15 times)
4. Romans 12:5—members of one another
5. Romans 12:10—kindly affection to one another
6. Romans 12:10—giving preference to one another
7. Romans 12:16—same mind toward one another
8. Romans 14:19- edify one another
9. Romans 15:7—receive one another
10. Romans 15:14—admonish one another

One-Another Ministry

11. Romans 16:16—greet one another
12. 1 Corinthians 11:33—wait for one another
13. 1 Corinthians 12:25—same care for one another
14. Galatians 5:13—through love serve one another
15. Galatians 6:2—bear one another's burdens
16. Ephesians 4:2—bearing with one another
17. Ephesians 4:32—be kind to one another
18. Ephesians 5:21—submitting to one another
19. Philippians 2:3—esteem one another better than self
20. 1 Thessalonians 4:18—comfort one another
21. 1 Thessalonians 5:15—follow that which is good for one another
22. Hebrews 10:24—consider one another to provoke unto love and to good works
23. James 5:16 –confess your faults one to another
24. James 5:16—pray for one another
25. 1 Peter 4:9—use hospitality one to another

There are also five with negative connotations:

1. Romans 14:13—let us not judge one another
2. 1 Corinthians 7:5—don't defraud one another
3. Colossians 3:9—Lie not to one another
4. James 4:11—speak not evil one to another
5. James 5:9—grudge not one against another

Bibliography

Anderson, Neil T. *Living Free in Christ*. Ventura: Regal Books, 1993.
Borthwick, Paul. *How to Be a World-Class Christian*. Wheaton: Victor Books, 1991.
Elliot, Elizabeth. *Through the Gates of Splendor*. Wheaton: Tyndale House, 1997.
Elwell, Walter A. *Evangelical Dictionary of Theology*. Grand Rapids: Baker Book House, 1984.
"Grace Greater than Our Sin." - HymnSite.com. January 1, 1911. Accessed September 2, 2014. http://www.hymnsite.com/lyrics/umh365.sht.
"Hunger and Poverty Fact Sheet." Feeding America. Accessed November 5, 2014.
"Hymn: When upon Life's Billows You Are Tempest Tossed." Hymnalnet RSS. Accessed May 8, 2014. http://www.hymnal.net/en/hymn/h/707#ixzz2xxANklyB.
"Keep Your Fork." Keep Your Fork. Accessed September 17, 2014. http://www.moytura.com/reflections/KeepYourFork.htm.
MacArthur, John. *The Love of God*. Dallas: Word Publishing, 1996.
MacArthur, John. *Safe in the Arms of God*. Nashville: Thomas Nelson, 2003.
MacArthur, John. *The MacArthur Study Bible: New King James Version*. Nashville: Word Bibles, 1997.
Marsh, F. E. *The Structural Principles of the Bible: Or, How to Study the Word of God*. Grand Rapids: Kregel Publications, 1969.
McDowell, Josh. *The New Evidence That Demands a Verdict*. [Rev., Updated, and Expanded]. ed. Nashville: T. Nelson, 1999.
"MillionsOfMouths.com - Website about Global Poverty and Hunger." Accessed October 1, 2014.
Ryrie, Charles. *Basic Theology*. Wheaton: Victor Books, 1986.
Shinabarger, Jeff. *More or Less: Choosing a Lifestyle of Excessive Generosity*. Colorado Springs: David C Cook, 2013.
"The Water Information Program | Providing Water Information to the Communities of Southwest Colorado." The Water Information Program | Providing Water Information to the Communities of Southwest Colorado. Accessed October 1, 2014. http://www.waterinfo.org.

Bibliography

"Two Traveling Angels Story for All Scouts." Accessed October 1, 2014. http://www.boyscouttrail.com/content/story/two_traveling_angels-196.asp.

Wallace, H. Webster. *I Heart Parenting*. Eugene: Resource Publications, 2012.

"Water Crisis." World Water Council. Accessed October 1, 2014. http://www.worldwatercouncil.org/library/archives/water-crisis/.

"What Is the 10/40 Window? :: Joshua Project." Accessed January 2, 2015.

"World Hunger Facts." Good Works Walk. Accessed September 2, 2014. http://www.goodworkswalk.net/world-hunger-facts/.

"Your Grace Finds Me" Lyrics. Matt Redman Lyrics. Accessed September 17, 2014. http://www.azlyrics.com/lyrics/mattredman/yourgracefindsme.html.

www.ingramcontent.com/pod-product-compliance
Lightning Source LLC
Chambersburg PA
CBHW071435160426
43195CB00013B/1914